THE 16 SIXTEEN PERSONALITY TYPES

Descriptions for Self-Discovery

LINDA V. BERENS   DARIO NARDI

Telos
PUBLICATIONS
Huntington Beach
CALIFORNIA

PRINTED IN CANADA

Myers-Briggs Type Indicator and *MBTI* are registered trademarks of Consulting Psychologists Press, Inc., Palo Alto, California.

Understanding Yourself and Others is a registered trademark of Telos Publications, Huntington Beach, California.

The Self-Discovery Process is a service mark of Temperament Research Institute, Huntington Beach, California.

Published By:
Telos Publications
P.O. Box 4457, Huntington Beach, California 92605-4457
714.668.1818 or 866.416.8973 / fax 714.668.1100
http://www.telospublications.com
International Standard Book Number: 0–9664624-7-5

03 02 01 00 99   10 9 8 7 6 5 4 3 2 1

Cover Photo: Oak and Beech Forest Reflected in Pond, Massachusetts, © 1998 Gary Braasch, Used with permission.
Cover/Layout Design/Illustrations: Visibility Designs, Fountain Valley, California – http://www.visibilitydesigns.com
Illustrations: Chris Berens of Thumbnail Productions, Austin, Texas

Ordering Information

Individual Sales U.S.: This publication can be purchased directly from the Telos Publications Web site or at the address above.

Individual Sales International: A list of international distributors can be received directly from the Telos Publications Web site or at the address above.

Quantity Sales: Special discounts are available on quantity purchases by corporations, associations, and others. Details can be received at the Telos Publications Web site or at the address above.

Orders for College Textbook/Course Adoption Use: Information can be received directly from the Telos Publications Web site or at the address above.

Orders by U.S./International Trade Bookstores and Wholesalers: Information can be received directly from the Telos Publications Web site or at the address above.

Training is available for further exploration of the information provided in this book.
Contact:
Temperament Research Institute (TRI)
http://www.tri-network.com
1-800-700-4TRI or 1-714-841-0041

TRI provides a certification curriculum for The TRI Methodology™ and The Self-Discovery Process™, organizational consulting and in-house training for communication, team building, leadership development, coaching, and organizational development, and is an approved provider of the Myers-Briggs Type Indicator® (MBTI®) Qualification Programs and MBTI Certification Continuing Education Programs. Please contact Temperament Research Institute (TRI) for a list of TRI-Certified providers.

A very special thanks to Vicky Jo Varner and Robin Wiley for helping to make this edition possible.

Acknowledgments

This book is dedicated to the sixty-four interviewees who gave generously of themselves and to all of the thousands who have talked freely about themselves in workshops and in conversations. Without you, this work would not exist.

Thanks from Linda to
- Katharine Myers, for getting me to look at Jung's work in terms of processes and for seeing value in my work.
- David Keirsey, for continuing to bring clarity to my understanding of people and introducing me to systems thinking.
- Margaret and Gary Hartzler, for their emphasis on the sixteen type patterns as where temperament and Jung's types meet.
- My husband, John, for the many nights, weekends, and holidays I wasn't really present and for his never-ending support.
- My family, Chris and Lynne Berens and Stephanie and Kris Kiler, for support, feedback, and dialogue.
- Stephanie Rogers, for the vision of these descriptions, the fifteen-plus months of interviews, and the risk she took of losing herself by "crawling inside" each type.

Thanks from Dario to
- Mike Dixon, for introducing me to type.
- My mom, Laura Power, for her intuition that a more in-depth understanding of type with Linda and TRI would be rewarding.
- Janet Schultz, who introduced me to the notion of internal strategies, which became a powerful tool for observing and exploring type.
- My sister, Sola Power, for countless hours of insights, discussions, and enthusiasm.
- My many students, who have provided me with a rich storehouse of data and opportunities to test my hypotheses and polish my type-watching skills.
- Prof. Walter Lowen, for providing the first link for me between artificial intelligence and type.
- Prof. Howard Pattee, for his tremendous and subtle insights into systems science, particularly the inexorable necessity of multiple "complementary" models.

Thanks from Temperament Research Institute to
- Colleagues, Linda Ernst and Melissa Smith for countless hours of feedback and input.
- The TRI-Network of professionals who gave us extensive feedback on the descriptions.

About
the Authors

Linda V. Berens

Linda V. Berens, Ph.D. is the Director and Founder of Temperament Research Institute, which provides organizational consulting, training and MBTI® qualifying programs. She is the author of *Understanding Yourself and Others™, an Introduction to Temperament*, and coauthor of *Working Together, a Personality Approach to Management* as well as numerous training materials. As an organizational development consultant, she applies systems thinking and understanding individual differences to solving organizational problems. She is a licensed Marriage and Family Therapist and Educational Psychologist, and has over twenty-five years experience using temperament and type with individuals and teaching these theories to professionals. Linda is recognized internationally for her contributions to the field of psychological type, for integrating temperament and Jung's typology, and for developing user friendly training materials for practical application of those theories.

Dario Nardi

Dario Nardi, Ph.D. is currently an Adjunct Assistant Professor of Mathematics at University of California, Los Angeles, in the department's Program in Computing. He has been working with type and temperament since 1992, and has been intimately involved in innovative product development with the Temperament Research Institute for seven years. He has authored several papers on type research with students. Dario received his degree in systems science from S.U.N.Y. Binghamton's Watson School of Engineering. His background in systems thinking, linguistics and artificial intelligence, undergraduate curriculum design and writing has led him to breakthroughs using multiple methods and models for getting at the "true self," as well as for restructuring academic courses to suit all learning styles.

Contents

From the Authors

Why We Wrote This Book

- To help more people better find their *best-fit type* and have an "aha" experience
- To incorporate advances in the field; share new developments in the theory; deepen understanding of the patterns; focus on systems thinking, type dynamics, and development rather than preferences alone
- To create descriptions that were written holistically from the "inside out" and not built from constructs
- To provide a tool for practitioners to facilitate accurate self-discovery

Design

The overall design of this book is based on the success of *Understanding Yourself and Others™, an Introduction to Temperament*. We wanted a product that worked with many learning styles, so we incorporated graphics, personal anecdotes, activities, a conceptual overview, an explanation of the theoretical frameworks (in Appendix A), and even an appendix for the facilitator/type-knowledgeable reader.

After an outline of The Self-Discovery Process℠, we present you with the themes of each type pattern. Each pattern is presented in three ways:

1. A very brief snapshot revolving mostly around roles and talents
2. A portrait that describes the themes from a third-person perspective
3. A self-portrait, written more in the spoken word from the first person than a formal written style. This self-portrait was developed from answers to the question, "What is it like to be you?" The four people of each type we interviewed were clear on their *best-fit type* pattern and "owned" the pattern.

History and Process

When Stephanie Rogers worked for Temperament Research Institute, she had the idea of creating descriptions based on how people of each type describe themselves. She conducted sixty-four interviews, reviewed the transcripts, and grouped the themes. The task was daunting—to integrate several "voices" and not insert her own voice into the narrative—and the task was put on hold.

Finally, the self-portraits were "born" from an interactive process. Linda Berens reviewed the transcripts of the interviews, and based on her twenty-five years of experience, lifted phrases and sentences that seemed to capture the essence of each type. Dario Nardi, with his background in script writing, put himself into each type from "the inside out" and with his eye for whole themes "composed" each description. A "theory check" insured our models of personality (temperament, interaction styles, and mental processes/type dynamics) were represented. We also needed third-person descriptions. From his background in systems science and Neuro Linguistic Programming, Dario identified essential "thematic processes" for each type. From these, Linda generated portraits, adding other aspects of the type to create a more parallel construction. Linda, Dario, and Kris Kiler generated the relationship pieces and refined them for relevancy and accuracy.

We field-tested the descriptions with type-knowledgeable people, our workshop participants, and members of our professional network and some of their clients. We found the descriptions worked well in helping people find their *best-fit type* pattern.

What We Learned

We are most appreciative of the richness and complexity of people. We learned that to be effective, the descriptions needed to have a psychological appeal to people of that type, not just accurately describe the categories. We *relearned* that it is hard to really get inside someone else's framework and also that as with most projects, everything takes longer than you imagine!

What We Hope

- These descriptions will help people launch an ongoing self-discovery process.
- You, the reader, will continue to give us feedback on what fits and what doesn't.

Whom We Thank

We thank all those who contributed, even though we can't name you all and have even lost track of some of you. This book would not exist without your willingness to self-disclose and dialogue about who you are and what is important to you.

Linda V. Berens   Dario Nardi
June 1999

What Is Personality?

Over the years, philosophers and behavioral scientists have been trying to find ways to understand what they call *personality*. *Personality* has many meanings. We like the definition given by Salvatore Maddi:

> *Personality is a stable set of characteristics and tendencies that determine those commonalities and differences in the psychological behavior (thoughts, feeling, and actions) of people that have continuity in time and that may not be easily understood as the sole result of the social and biological pressures of the moment.**

> There are so many models to explain personality. How can all these models be right? Which one is the best? Isn't there a way to take the best of each of them and not waste a lot of time and effort?

Personality typing is popular. Most widely used models ultimately describe sixteen discrete patterns. This booklet provides descriptions that represent the best of all these models. These sixteen type descriptions are not derived from a single framework such as social styles, Keirsey's four temperaments, the Myers-Briggs types, or Jung. They are descriptive of sixteen universal themes that exist in and of themselves, yet reflect all of the above frameworks.

> It's good to consider multiple models! You can't know the whole by looking at just the parts. There must be a universal theme. Furthermore, what are the assumptions behind personality?

Historically, professionals have alternated between the idea that personality is inborn and the seemingly opposite view that it results from our experiences. The most current thinking is that personality is both inborn *and* conditioned by the environment.

> Now wait a minute! I am free to act according to the needs of the moment. So how can there be anything "determined" about that? Don't put me in a box!

Personality Has Several Aspects

The Contextual Self

The contextual self is who we are in any given environment. It is how we behave depending on what the situation requires. The idea of a personality "type" doesn't leave out freedom of action in the moment.

The Developed Self

When the contextual self becomes habitual and ongoing, it becomes a part of the developed self. Personality development is influenced by our choices and decisions (free will) as well as by interactions and roles (social field theory).

> I'm glad you recognize people are unique and they grow and develop. We can't limit our potential by stereotyping people!

The True Self

An aspect of our personality exists from the beginning of our lives. This aspect of ourselves is in our genes, our DNA. We are born with a *tendency* to behave in certain ways, which influences how we adapt, grow and develop.

When looking at personality types, all three of these aspects must be considered. Current behavior and adaptations may or may not be consistent with the true self. All are interrelated.

> Personality is complex, and several descriptions may fit different aspects of you. We hope this booklet helps you find the pattern closest to your true self—your best-fit type pattern.

*Salvatore R. Maddi, *Personality Theories: A Comparative Analysis*, 3d ed. (Homewood, Ill.: The Dorsey Press, 1976), p. 9.

Understanding Personality

What Is Personality "Type"?

Personality typing has been around for over twenty-five centuries. It seems we have a natural tendency to categorize so that we can understand and remember. When we were infants learning to talk, we called every furry animal a dog or a cat, depending on which name we happened to learn first. Later, we were able to see the differences between a dog, a cat and a bunny. These categories and names became our models for the world and shape our perception and thus our expectations. We make assumptions and inferences about the nature of things based on these prior learnings.

> Look at the three ovals below.
> What do they represent?
> Ovals or manholes or shadows or ???

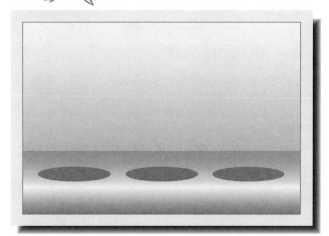

> If we tell you they are shadows,
> what are they shadows of?

> The most frequently given answer
> is that they are shadows of a ball or
> sphere. Of course, by now you have looked
> at the next graphic and seen that they are
> shadows made by different shapes.

> Notice what the three objects
> have in common—they are circular in
> some way. Knowing about the different
> personality type patterns can also help you
> see some qualities you have in common with
> friends, family, and coworkers.

Personality type patterns are like these shadows. When trying to understand personality, all we have to judge a person by is outer behavior—we don't see the motivation behind the behavior. People can display the same behavior for very different reasons. Therefore, it is important to not overgeneralize and make assumptions, yet it is useful to make guesses and hypotheses. Knowing which type pattern fits you best can help you understand what is behind your outer behavior. Knowing about the patterns of your friends, family, and coworkers can help you meet them at their view of the world, rather than just reacting to their outer behavior.

The context or situation is also important in determining what behavior we engage in. We are not limited by our personality "types." The *best-fit type* pattern is the one we "prefer," the one that comes most naturally to us and that we are most likely to practice and develop. We can remain flexible and adaptable. Sometimes the environmental context can make figuring out who we are confusing because we look like one pattern in one setting and another in other settings.

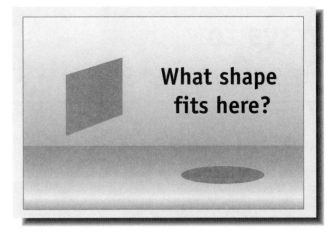

For the different shapes to cast the same shadows, the light has to be at a certain angle. If we change the light, we see a differently shaped shadow.

If we can see both shadows instead of just one, we can more accurately infer which shape is making the shadows. So to really understand someone's personality, we need multiple perspectives.

Humans are very complex and cannot be understood in terms of a few simple formulas, yet there are some simple, easy-to-comprehend principles or dynamics that help us understand ourselves and others. Fritjof Capra* has said that to understand any "living system" you have to look at the *pattern*, the *processes,* and the *structure* of the system. To Capra's principles we add *purpose*.

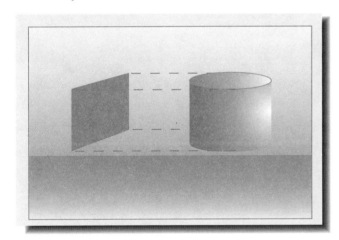

Personality can be seen as a living system.

Different people of different "types" can engage in the same behavior. Type does not always predict or determine behavior.

Pattern—The interrelationships within a system. Every system, including personality, is defined by essential characteristics. These are the qualities that must exist, such as the trunk, roots, or branches of a tree. The characteristics are interrelated, and the configuration of relationships is the pattern, like the way the trunk, roots, and branches of a tree are related.
Processes—The activities the system engages in as it functions in day-to-day life and as it grows.
Structure—How the pattern is physically expressed.
Purpose—The holistic theme of the pattern.

Knowing the "Self"

Personalities cannot be measured, they can only be mapped. You cannot describe a person in any definite and specific way since the person is constantly changing, adapting, and evolving. Any one perspective or shadow shape will give only one data point. When mapping a personality, we can make only approximate measurements, so we "triangulate," or see where several indicators from multiple models meet. Then we have a good idea of what the personality is like.

When all of these perspectives intersect in the same "place," we can be more sure we have accurately described the true self.

*Fritjof Capra, *The Web of Life: A New Scientific Understanding of Living Systems* (New York, NY.: Anchor Books, 1996)

Ways to Describe Personality

Traits and Parts

Personality can be described in many ways. The most common approaches include observing and *measuring* traits like cheerfulness, anxiety, and outgoingness. Sometimes the traits are extremely relevant to a particular job performance, so there is value to this approach. However, even when there is an attempt to see a pattern to the traits, the result is usually a fragmented picture that gives little useful information.

> This approach is a little bit like trying to understand a tree by looking at its parts. You will learn something about the tree but won't know how it works or why it works. You may not even recognize the tree unless you already know what a tree looks like.

Parts have meaning only in reference to the whole.

Processes and Parts

Other times personality is described by looking at separate dynamic processes, such as how we gather information and make decisions. This is not purely a trait approach because no attempt is made to measure the degree of the trait, but the processes are often treated as separate parts that somehow combine with each other. Processes, however, have meaning only in reference to the whole context, so descriptions based only on this approach are often missing essential qualities.

> This is like describing how trees process moisture without considering that different kinds of trees process moisture somewhat differently.

Systems

Living systems are not concretely visible. Only in the last forty years have behavioral scientists really been learning to "see" systems, especially human systems.

Systems are patterns of relationships that are organized.

Systems have "rules" that govern their behavior. The pattern of organization is not imposed from outside but "comes with" the system at the moment of creation. The system is organized around a deep operating principle.

Systems are "driven" to operate in certain ways. If we try to force a system to behave in ways inconsistent with its nature, we spend energy and encounter resistance. If we can understand the inherent operating principles and work with them, we can save energy. Personality descriptions using a systems approach try to portray the system as a whole.

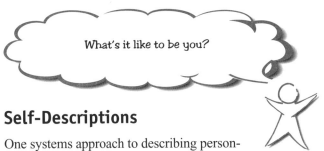

What's it like to be you?

Self-Descriptions

One systems approach to describing personality is to have people describe themselves. Unfortunately, people are influenced by the models they already have, as well as their self-esteem, traumas, stress and cultures, so they may describe themselves in a somewhat limited way. However, people and the inborn patterns existed before any theoretical models, so the expressions of self-esteem, traumas, stress, and culture will themselves be influenced by the push of that inborn pattern.

Since each type pattern is reflected in language, such an approach can use the language of the type, its syntax, vocabulary, rhythm, and so on. Descriptions developed this way can be very helpful in self-discovery, even if they do not comprehensively describe the theory.

Type Themes and Patterns

A second way of describing personality using a systems approach is to describe personality in terms of the themes of each type pattern and how they are organized. This approach portrays aspects not available any other way.

**Each of the sixteen types is a
pattern of related themes.**

It reveals the pattern of the various dynamics at play. Sometimes it is hard to sort out what is the essence of the theme and what is culture or the result of growth and development. Yet the pattern of themes is constant under varying conditions.

**The themes describe processes that
fill a unique role for each type.**

The sixteen themes and patterns reflect internal processes as well as interactions with the environment. This is like looking at a tree and recognizing the interrelationships of the parts of the tree and the role of the tree in the larger environment.

About the Descriptions in This Book

The descriptions are designed to help people sort out which of the sixteen type patterns is the *best-fit* for them. They are not comprehensive descriptions. Neither are they driven by a single theory or model. They are whole type descriptions, based on themes unique to that type.

We have found different people find themselves better through different kinds of descriptions. For example, seeing the brief description worked better for some people. For others, the third-person description was all they wanted, and they found the first-person description irrelevant. Yet for many, the first-person description was what helped them the most. As one person put it, "You've reached into my reality." Most found the three approaches taken together worked best.

- **The brief snapshot** briefly describes the roles and talents of the type.
- **The third-person portrait** describes the themes of the type and the theme in relationships.
- **The first-person self-portraits** are based on interviews with at least two men and two women of each type who were asked, "What is it like to be you?" The content is based on the themes of what they spontaneously offered as most relevant to who they are. In the self-portraits we tried to keep as true as possible to their *spoken voice*, using their words and phrases.

How to Discover Your *Best-Fit Type*

What Is *Best-Fit Type*?

Best-fit type refers to the type pattern that fits you best. No one description or pattern will be a perfect match to all of who you are. Your personality is rich and complex, and a "type" or type pattern cannot adequately express all of that richness. Each of the sixteen types comes in a variety of "flavors," and *best-fit type* means that the themes and preferred processes of that type seem to fit you the best.

Personality Instruments

> *"Not everything that counts can be counted; and not everything that can be counted counts."*
> — Albert Einstein

Sometimes people come to understand who they are through self-reporting on personality instruments. No instruments that rely solely on self-reporting are completely accurate. They must all be accompanied by a validation process, preferably involving self-discovery. Many instruments have standards that require face-to-face facilitated feedback with a qualified professional. This booklet is not meant to replace this valuable interactive process but to support it.

Personality instruments that are well researched and well designed can help us tune in to key aspects of who we are. They are designed to reveal ourselves to ourselves. The Myers-Briggs Type Indicator® (MBTI®) was developed to suggest possible *best-fit type* patterns. While the MBTI is one of the more thoroughly researched instruments and is widely used, it is sometimes not 100 percent accurate on all four of the letters that are use to summarize personality characteristics.

As you read this booklet, allow yourself to "try on" more than one type pattern to see which one fits you the best. If you have had exposure to instruments like the MBTI, set aside any assumptions you have about your *best-fit type* pattern.

In any case, any one model—like temperament or the MBTI®—is frequently insufficient to reveal one's personality pattern by itself. This is why we recommend the use of multiple models in The Self-Discovery Process℠—with or without a personality instrument.

> An instrument will not tell you who you are, it can only indicate who you might be.

The Self-Discovery Process℠

One powerful way to find your *best-fit type* pattern is through self-discovery. This works very well for many people.

Self-Reflection

The Johari Window,* originally used for improving communication, is a useful map to help us understand this self-discovery process.

For example, one area is "Public Knowledge"— what we know about ourselves and is known to others around us. These "public" aspects of ourselves are easily recognized. What do we talk about over coffee or around the water cooler? Discovering how we communicate in

The Johari Window

	Known to Self	Unknown to Self
Known to Others	**Public Knowledge . . .** *What I Show You*	**Feedback . . .** *Your Gift to Me*
Unknown to Others	**Private . . .** *Mine to Share*	**Unconscious . . .** *Not to Probe but I Can Become More Aware and Choose to Share*

general is one part of getting in touch with who we really are. Listen to what you say and how you say it. What do you *like* to talk about? These topics will likely reflect your natural self. Be aware that your public self may reflect adaptive or learned behavior. This adaptive self is also part of who you are but may not hold the key to what energizes you.

---

*Originally formulated by Joseph Luft and Harry Ingham in "The Johari Window, A Graphic Model of Awareness in Interpersonal Relations." pp. 10-12, in *Group Process: An Introduction to Group Dynamics* by Joseph Luft, Palo Alto: National Press Books, 1963.

Interaction with Others— Sharing and Feedback

We also learn who we are through our interactions with others. Finding people who are similar to us and comparing notes and sharing stories helps many of us discover our own *best-fit type* pattern. This often happens in workshops when people openly discuss their type patterns in order to better understand themselves and others. Sometimes this kind of discussion takes us into the "Private" area of the Johari Window—those aspects known to ourselves and not known to others. In the same way, self-discovery often sends us to this area, at least privately.

One valuable way of finding out who we are is by actively seeking feedback—asking others to tell us how they see us. These people may be trained facilitators or merely people who know us well. The "Feedback" area of the Johari Window gives us the opportunity to learn about those aspects of ourselves unknown to us but known to others. This provides additional information as we explore who we are. And remember, this feedback is a gift, often given through the eyes of the giver—so seek feedback from many people.

Openness to New Information

During The Self-Discovery Process℠ "Unconscious" information sometimes comes into our minds—aspects previously unknown to ourselves and unknown to others. The unconscious is often where we "store" information about how to "be" in the world. As you explore who you are, stay open to valuable insights from this area.

Many variables may be involved in your self-discovery process. Be aware that family, social, cultural, and other influences will affect how you view yourself in relation to the type patterns. These influences are often unconscious until they somehow come into our awareness when they are described and pointed out. Stay open and searching. Seek input from all areas of the Johari Window.

Descriptions for Self-Discovery

A Word about Words!

In writing the descriptions, we have chosen various words to try to capture the themes of each type pattern. These words often reflect the way people with this type pattern think of themselves as well as the deep theoretical underpinnings. Words are subject to individual interpretations with various connotations, so beware the one-word category! One or two words cannot capture the whole of a pattern. The words were tested with many people, but they are not the last word! Don't let the meaning you may find in any one word or phrase prevent you from considering the pattern as a whole.

The Names of the Patterns

We've given names to the patterns in order to emphasize that the type is more than the sum of its parts or any single model. Names can more easily represent themes and also make the pattern more personal and real.

There is also a logic behind the names. The first word in the name is the inside view:

- How we often see ourselves
- What others often don't see

The second word in the name is the outside view:

- How others often see us
- What we may not see in ourselves

The words work together, each enriching and clarifying the meaning of the other, reflecting most of the theoretical models behind the descriptions.

Sixteen type patterns are a lot of patterns to try on. Many people learn which patterns are the ones that fit them the best through a facilitated process. However, you may be exploring on your own, so here are some handy hints.

Four Easy Steps

1. Look at the map on the next two pages and see which type themes are like you.*

2. Rule out any patterns that obviously do not fit.

3. Pick several to read in depth.

4. Look at page 11 for other suggested pattern descriptions to read.

---

*The pattern names are listed with the MBTI® four-letter codes for the convenience of those who use them.

Foreseer Developer • INFJ, Page 38

Personal growth. Sustain the vision. Honoring the gifts of others. Taking a creative approach to life. Talent for foreseeing. Exploring issues. Bridge differences and connect people. Practical problem solving. Live with a sense of purpose. Living an idealistic life often presents them with a great deal of stress and a need to withdraw.

Harmonizer Clarifier • INFP, Page 42

Going with the flow. Knowing what is behind what is said. Uncovering mysteries. Exploring moral questions. Talent for facilitative listening. Relate through stories and metaphors. Balancing opposites. Getting reacquainted with themselves. Have a way of knowing what is believable. Struggling with structure and getting their lives in order.

IDEALIST THEMES

Envisioner Mentor • ENFJ, Page 36

Communicate and share values. Succeeding at relationships. Realizing dreams—their own and others. Seek opportunities to grow together. Heeding the call to a life work or mission. Enjoy the creative process. Intuitive intellect. Reconcile the past and the future. Talent for seeing potential in others. Often find living in the present difficult.

Discoverer Advocate • ENFP, Page 40

Inspiring and facilitating others. Exploring perceptions. Talent for seeing what's not being said and voicing unspoken meanings. Seek to have ideal relationships. Recognize happiness. Living out stories. Want to authentically live with themselves. Respond to insights in the creative process. Finding the magical situation. Restless hunger for discovering their direction.

Conceptualizer Director • INTJ, Page 30

Maximizing achievements. Drive for self-mastery. Build a vision. Very long-range strategizing. Realizing progress toward goals. Systems thinking. Talent for seeing the reasons behind things. Being on the leading edge. Maintaining independence. Find it difficult to let go in interacting with others.

Designer Theorizer • INTP, Page 34

Becoming an expert. Seeing new patterns and elegant connections. Talent for design and redesign. Crossing the artificial boundaries of thought. Activate the imagination. Clarifying and defining. Making discoveries. Reflect on the process of thinking itself. Detach to analyze. Struggle with attending to the physical world.

RATIONAL THEMES

Strategist Mobilizer • ENTJ, Page 28

Being a leader. Maximize talents. Marshal resources toward progress. Intuitive explorations. Forging partnerships. Mentoring and empowering. Talent for coordinating multiple projects. Balance peace and conflict. Predictive creativity. Often overwhelmed by managing all the details of time and resources.

Explorer Inventor • ENTP, Page 32

Being inventive. Talented at building prototypes and getting projects launched. Lifelong learning. Enjoy the creative process. Share their insights about life's possibilities. Strategically formulate success. An inviting host. Like the drama of the give and take. Trying to be diplomatic. Surprised when their strategizing of relationships becomes problematic.

Planner Inspector • ISTJ, Page 22

Drawing up plans and being prepared. Take responsibility. Getting work done first. Being active in the community. Loyalty to their roles. Cultivating good qualities. Doing the right thing. Bear life's burdens and overcome adversity. Talented at planning, sequencing, and noticing what's missing. Having to learn so much in hindsight is painful at times.

Protector Supporter • ISFJ, Page 26

Noticing what's needed and what's valuable. Talent for careful and supportive organization. Know the ins and outs. Enjoy traditions. Work to protect the future. Listening and remembering. Being nice and agreeable. Unselfish willingness to volunteer. Feeling a sense of accomplishment. Exasperated when people ignore rules and don't get along.

GUARDIAN THEMES

Implementor Supervisor • ESTJ, Page 20

Talent for bringing order to chaotic situations. Educating themselves. Industrious, work-hard attitude. Balance work with play. Having a philosophy of life. Having the steps to success. Keeping up traditions. Being well balanced. Connecting their wealth of life experiences. Often disappointed when perfectionistic standards for economy and quality are not met.

Facilitator Caretaker • ESFJ, Page 24

Accepting and helping others. Managing people. Hearing people out. Voicing concerns and accommodating needs. Admire the success of others. Remember what's important. Talented at providing others with what they need. Keep things pleasant. Maintaining a sense of continuity. Accounting for the costs. Often disappointed by entrepreneurial projects.

Analyzer Operator • ISTP, Page 14

Actively solving problems. Observing how things work. Talent for using tools for the best approach. Need to be independent. Act on their hunches or intuitions. Understanding a situation. Taking things apart. Making discoveries. Sharing those discoveries. Unsettled by powerful emotional experiences.

Composer Producer • ISFP, Page 18

Taking advantage of opportunities. Stick with what's important. Talent for pulling together what is just right. Creative problem solving. Building relationships. Attracting the loyalties of others. Being their own true self. Have their own personal style. Play against expectations. Struggle with nurturing their own self-esteem.

ARTISAN THEMES

Promoter Executor • ESTP, Page 12

Taking charge of situations. Tactical prioritizing. Talent for negotiating. Want a measure of their success. Keep their options open. Enjoy acting as a consultant. Winning people over. Caring for family and friends. Enjoy exhilaration at the edge. Disappointed when others don't show respect.

Motivator Presenter • ESFP, Page 16

Stimulating action. Have a sense of style. Talent for presenting things in a useful way. Natural actors—engaging others. Opening up people to possibilities. Respect for freedom. Taking risks. A love of learning, especially about people. Genuine caring. Sometimes misperceive others' intentions.

Experiencing the Descriptions

In testing the descriptions, we received a variety of responses. Most people found them helpful in finding their *best-fit type*. People who have read the descriptions made comments such as

- "How could you know so much about me?"
- "This was right on!"
- "I could have written this myself!"
- "This is the best description of my type I have seen."

Yet some people had mixed responses. Those who already knew about psychological type were often looking for descriptions based on a single model or other models they already had seen. We hope you allow this new learning opportunity to open you up to re-exploring your own type and perhaps an even better fit.

You may relate to some aspects of the descriptions more than other aspects. Younger people may not have encountered some issues yet, and some of those who are older may have already transcended some of those issues. Also, people with the same type patterns emphasize different themes within their patterns. It's natural for individuals to not connect with everything in a description. Respond to the description as a whole. Remember, each type pattern has many "flavors."

A few people may not find a perfect fit with just one description. Most often, these people will have adapted over time to stress and different environments. Also, it is natural for certain types of people to find themselves in multiple descriptions. Alas, no theory is perfect! Our experience is that eventually most people can find their *best-fit type* without denying the gifts of their adaptations. Give yourself some time to reflect and get feedback.

> Stay open and "try on" several types. Based on our experiences with helping people clarify their best-fit type pattern, it is important for you to actively interact with the descriptions by
> - accepting aspects that ring true and rejecting aspects that don't
> - seeking feedback from others
> - reflecting on what you've read

How to Experience the Descriptions

> A song can make your heart sing,
> it can move you to express yourself,
> or it may leave you cold,
> or even offend.
>
> When you hear it,
> and it's for you,
> then it rings true
> and feels good.
>
> If it doesn't speak to you,
> it may still be a good song,
> just not your song.

> Self-discovery is like listening to a song. You listen to it as a whole. If you separate or rearrange the notes or change the rhythm or the sequence, you lose the melody. Remember to listen to the whole description. See how it feels. Does it feel right? Is it your song?

Your Self-Discovery

For the best chance of accurate type identification, we advise you to read more than one description. More than one of the descriptions may be more or less true of you, but only one is likely to really "make your heart sing" and therefore be your "best fit." If you have decided to consider a particular type pattern based on an instrument like the Myers-Briggs Type Indicator® or the Keirsey Sorter, please remember that no personality instrument or single model is completely accurate in identifying your type pattern. Read other, related descriptions.

Discover yourself and others

Helping You Decide

After reviewing the themes on pages 8-9, use the matrix on the right to

• Cross out the ones that are not like you.

• Then, of the ones left, check out the themes that appeal to you.

Be sure to think of yourself in all contexts, not just at work or at home. Who are you really?

❑ INFJ Page 38	❑ INFP Page 42	❑ ISTJ Page 22	❑ ISFJ Page 26
❑ ENFJ Page 36	❑ ENFP Page 40	❑ ESTJ Page 20	❑ ESFJ Page 24
❑ INTJ Page 30	❑ INTP Page 34	❑ ISTP Page 14	❑ ISFP Page 18
❑ ENTJ Page 28	❑ ENTP Page 32	❑ ESTP Page 12	❑ ESFP Page 16

About the Other Suggested Patterns

Some of these patterns are genuine "look-alikes" for various logical reasons. Our experiences in facilitating The Self-Discovery Process^{SM} with thousands of people have led us to suggest other patterns that are not "logical." Most often these are based on ways certain types experience the process or respond to instruments. For the same reasons, not every type has the same number of suggestions.

Other Suggested Patterns to Read

Foreseer Developer • INFJ
also consider

Envisioner Mentor	•	ENFJ—p. 36
Conceptualizer Director	•	INTJ—p. 30
Harmonizer Clarifier	•	INFP—p. 42

Harmonizer Clarifier • INFP
also consider

Discoverer Advocate	•	ENFP—p. 40
Composer Producer	•	ISFP—p. 18

Planner Inspector • ISTJ
also consider

Implementor Supervisor	•	ESTJ—p. 20
Protector Supporter	•	ISFJ—p. 26
Analyzer Operator	•	ISTP—p. 14

Protector Supporter • ISFJ
also consider

Facilitator Caretaker	•	ESFJ—p. 24
Planner Inspector	•	ISTJ—p. 22

IDEALIST / **GUARDIAN**

Envisioner Mentor • ENFJ
also consider

Foreseer Developer	•	INFJ—p. 38
Facilitator Caretaker	•	ESFJ—p. 24
Promoter Executor	•	ESTP—p. 12
Motivator Presenter	•	ESFP—p. 16

Discoverer Advocate • ENFP
also consider

Harmonizer Clarifier	•	INFP—p. 42
Explorer Inventor	•	ENTP—p. 32
Motivator Presenter	•	ESFP—p. 16
Promoter Executor	•	ESTP—p. 12

Implementor Supervisor • ESTJ
also consider

Planner Inspector	•	ISTJ—p. 22
Strategist Mobilizer	•	ENTJ—p. 28
Promoter Executor	•	ESTP—p. 12

Facilitator Caretaker • ESFJ
also consider

Protector Supporter	•	ISFJ—p. 26
Envisioner Mentor	•	ENFJ—p. 36
Motivator Presenter	•	ESFP—p. 16

Conceptualizer Director • INTJ
also consider

Strategist Mobilizer	•	ENTJ—p. 28
Foreseer Developer	•	INFJ—p. 38
Analyzer Operator	•	ISTP—p. 14
Designer Theorizer	•	INTP—p. 34

Designer Theorizer • INTP
also consider

Explorer Inventor	•	ENTP—p. 32
Analyzer Operator	•	ISTP—p. 14
Harmonizer Clarifier	•	INFP—p. 42
Conceptualizer Director	•	INTJ—p. 30

Analyzer Operator • ISTP
also consider

Promoter Executor	•	ESTP—p. 12
Conceptualizer Director	•	INTJ—p. 30

Composer Producer • ISFP
also consider

Motivator Presenter	•	ESFP—p. 16
Harmonizer Clarifier	•	INFP—p. 42

RATIONAL / **ARTISAN**

Strategist Mobilizer • ENTJ
also consider

Conceptualizer Director	•	INTJ—p. 30
Implementor Supervisor	•	ESTJ—p. 20
Promoter Executor	•	ESTP—p. 12

Explorer Inventor • ENTP
also consider

Designer Theorizer	•	INTP—p. 34
Discoverer Advocate	•	ENFP—p. 40
Promoter Executor	•	ESTP—p. 12

Promoter Executor • ESTP
also consider

Analyzer Operator	•	ISTP—p. 14
Motivator Presenter	•	ESFP—p. 16

Presenter Motivator • ESFP
also consider

Composer Producer	•	ISFP—p. 18
Promoter Executor	•	ESTP—p. 12

Promoter Executor

TEMPERAMENT: ARTISAN
INTERACTION STYLE: IN-CHARGE
PERSONALITY TYPE CODE: ESTP

SNAPSHOT

Theme is promoting. Talents lie in persuading others and expediting to make things happen. Have an engaging, winning style that others are drawn to. Adept at picking up on minimal nonverbal cues. Anticipate the actions and reactions of others and thus win their confidence. Like the excitement and challenge of negotiating, selling, making deals, arbitrating, and in general, achieving the impossible. Thrive on action and the freedom to use all resources at hand to get desired outcomes.

PORTRAIT

Themes

For Promoter Executors, life is a process of taking charge of situations and making things happen. They enjoy a certain exhilaration at the edge, pushing the limits to get the results they want. Then they want to know the measure of their success. Achieving success drives them to work hard, and they want recognition for their success as well as the rewards.

They go to great lengths to keep their options open. The freedom to act is essential to their well-being. Constraints and limits become challenges to work around, but too many of them can be deadly. They are talented at tactical prioritizing. Everything gets subordinated to their priorities as they "stay the course" to do what needs doing. Yet when they see something isn't working the way they want, they do not hesitate to change their approach or even abandon the project entirely.

Their thought processes tend to revolve around continuously scanning the environment for relevant information, opportunities, and resources, then quickly adjusting their behavior. Then action is taken—over and done, results achieved or adaptations made—all with split-second timing.

Their talent for negotiating shows in how easily they work different sides of an issue. They quickly find the bargaining points and the bottom lines, recognizing when to push and when to back off. Their rich stores of data—places, people, dates—often prompt them to act as a consultant, even when the project or problem isn't theirs. They love it if they can help solve a challenging problem.

They are keen observers of others' nonverbal responses and reactions, instantly seeing what people are up to. Their humor, enthusiasm, and direct approach win people over. Interpersonally, people warm to them quickly. People are important to them. Caring for family and friends comes through in how they pitch in and help.

Showing respect is important. Their talent for reading people's motives sometimes keeps them from showing respect when it is expected. It also leads them to disappointment when others don't show respect.

Relationships

For Promoter Executors, relationships are about mutual respect. There's no relationship if they can't respect the other person. What makes the respect is that the other person doesn't try to put anything over on them, the other person gives them the freedom to act, and whether they win or lose the other person sees that and still supports them. They like excitement and stimulation and can get a lot out of conflict. There is an admiration of skill in the other person, especially if the person has a unique talent or skill. They like a willingness on the other person's part to do things for them. They have an attitude that gets people to follow along; they can get people to do what they want, a way that communicates, "I'm your friend, so do this for me." There is a certain element of power and a devotedness, protecting your own.

In their close relationships, they desire somebody to connect with and have fun with, somebody to talk to. They want companionship, somebody to just be with. They also need a great deal of latitude and want a say in running the relationship. They tend to be extremely generous with material possessions, but can tend to avoid the personal. They may end up with the perception that the other person is letting them down when in fact *they* haven't put in the time and effort. When they do, they become really family oriented, and when family is very important to them, they take it very seriously.

SELF-PORTRAIT
From Conversations with Promoter Executors

What's it like to be you?

I make it happen. How I work—I have a picture in my head on how things will be, and I'm totally involved in the here and now. I am go, go, go. And that creates a lot of successes. I just dodge my way through the sparks and problems. I'm very task oriented. I like to do something, get it done, and move to the next thing. I love circumstances where it's a challenge.

I'm a doer. What's the mission and how are we getting there? Let's work together. Let's go. Throw any obstacle, I'll find a way.

New stuff, that's the thrill. I love to learn. I can take a prior experience and lay it right on top of what I'm doing today and carry it all forward, and it's a snap. I do a lot of brainstorming on my feet, organizing the points in my mind mentally. What's to worry? Just adapt. But draw me a picture, get me a list, or put it on my calendar. Sitting still is hard for me. I am really activity oriented and I don't need lots of supervision. I look for variety in most positions. If it's not there, I tend not to stay. I'd rather go out there and do it, just get on with things, and I can communicate that without having to spend a lot of time explaining. People know that if I have something that needs to be done, I do it. And I ask for help when it's needed.

I am totally a people person. Working through people is the way to get things done. All of my energy, fun, and most uplifting experiences are focused around people. I don't beat around the bush. Sometimes I have to tone it down a little bit—people may read me the wrong way. I'm very comfortable working either together as a team or individually. I like having flexibility, options, negotiating points. Some people need somebody to be very clear, very direct, and very to the point. That's how I operate. And work needs to be mutually enjoyable for all of the parties involved. Celebrate achievements. Recognition or reward runs very high in my value system.

I love the challenge of creating something pleasing to the eye. I like the order, to walk into a place that's totally chaotic, nothing's happening, and there's a great opportunity to straighten things out. I like to get the job of placing all the stuff, making it right so it works.

I like somebody with a little sizzle. The most important thing in relationships is absolute autonomy and independence. I admit I like to be in control and yet I'm kind of easygoing in that I just want freedom. Freedom to me is leave me alone, let me do it. Anything that constrains me around that I don't like and kind of rebel against. I don't like to be told what to do or what to think. And although I know it's good for me, I don't like feedback either. It takes a lot to rattle me, and even then I just go on. I tend not to dwell on things, but sometimes I have a tendency to imagine worst-case scenarios, especially when I am stressed.

Family is very important. Just getting together and being close with the family, I think that's satisfying. I don't have a whole lot of really deep friendships, but yet I like to think people would describe me as dedicated, determined, and loyal. I sometimes have difficulty concealing what I am thinking or feeling. I don't like the pressure of having to say no. I can be somewhat cool but a genuine friend as a personal relationship evolves. Trustworthiness in personal relationships is very important, that we can disagree and still be friends, and if our backs were ever to the wall, I'm there and I would expect the same.

If I don't respect someone, I avoid them. If I can find another way to do business I will. I surround myself with people that I feel comfortable with, but they're totally my selection.

I like taking on something that I want to do and getting it done and seeing results, keeping things moving along just to see that I have met some goals—a feeling of accomplishment in a day. I'll always take bigger risks if I feel confident enough. Then I'll work with it for a while, and if I see it's not going anywhere, I just move on and go from there. I guess that summarizes how I deal with situations.

Analyzer Operator

TEMPERAMENT: ARTISAN
INTERACTION STYLE: CHART THE COURSE
PERSONALITY TYPE CODE: ISTP

SNAPSHOT

Theme is action-driven problem solving. Talents lie in operating all kinds of tools and instruments and using frameworks for solving problems. Keen observers of the environment, they are a storehouse of data and facts relevant to analyzing and solving problems. Thrive on challenging situations and having the freedom to craft clever solutions and do whatever it takes to fix things and make them work. Take pride in their skill and virtuosity, which they seem to effortlessly acquire.

PORTRAIT

Themes

For Analyzer Operators, life is a process of actively solving problems. They enjoy observing how things work, figuring out the best way to solve whatever problem is at hand. That problem might be as basic as fixing something broken or as extensive as heart surgery or starting a business. They have a talent for figuring out what tools to use and the best approach to take to accomplish something. They want to do it so it works the first time and hate having to rework something.

They need to be independent, to do things on their own or to be free to not do them. To not have the freedom to act on their hunches or intuitions is a fate worse than death since it means not using their tactical, problem-solving talent.

Naturally curious, they seek to understand a situation, frequently analyzing and taking things apart to figure out how they work. Then they quickly grasp the most expedient solution, one that will fix it. Once they figure out the immediate next step, they want to move on it, see what happens, and then move on to the next challenge. Others see the fearless, just-do-it attitude and miss the analysis behind the scenes.

Their thought processes tend to be analytical and observational. They quickly scan the environment for inconsistencies, changes, and new information. Then they adapt and work around whatever obstacles appear. And they rarely work on just one thing at a time. No theory or explanation is accepted as the "truth" as there are always more discoveries to make, ways to do it better. They enjoy sharing those discoveries, showing others the techniques that work and the shortcuts that keep things simple. They don't like change just for change sake, but they do like variety.

In the interpersonal arena, they like to help people solve problems and frequently are called on for help in fixing things. They engage more by doing things with those they care about than by expressions of feeling.

For the most part, they go to great lengths to keep situations on an even keel, to not offend. They sometimes absorb emotional experiences that can often have a very powerful effect on them. This can be unsettling until they can detach enough to figure it all out.

Relationships

For Analyzer Operators, relationships are about taking action. Relationships often center on problem solving, and solving problems for others is how they show they care. They want to feel pride in doing something concrete for the other person, doing whatever uses their talents. They often feel a need to feel smart, and they admire people who are smart. Generally, they are very independent and will resist outside direction, wanting to do things the way they've figured out is the best way. They know how to do it, don't want others to tell them how, and can be critical and sarcastic if overdirected. If they don't feel trapped, they'll stick with the relationship and can be very loyal. Unlike in other aspects of their lives, they like having a routine in relationships. Establishing a relationship can take a lot of energy, so once it's done, it can take a lot of energy to change it. They want the other person to be straightforward with them in communication.

In their close relationships, they are generally good providers and helpmates. They prefer to be with people who share their interests or else allow them to "do their own thing." They don't like to talk through interpersonal problems in terms of their feelings. Displays of strong emotions can be taken very seriously and then overwhelm them. Sitting down and talking out their emotions makes them feel trapped. They show how they care more through their actions than their words.

SELF-PORTRAIT
From Conversations with Analyzer Operators

What's it like to be you?

Inside I am continually reworking an issue. I am constantly open to new directions, always tweaking and bringing in new information. I solve a problem by looking at all the angles, probably whatever side I need to. There is an answer, and I just need to get to the best way to figure it out—to meet my objectives and give it to people how it is without annoying anyone.

To work with difficult situations I become very logical and very analytical, and I look to see where things fit. I always watch and if there's a problem, I go back inside myself to see what may need to be done and how best to approach a situation. I like to find a technique.

The observational part of me is the ability to see when an opportunity exists and to actually act on it and make things a little bit better. I like to choose the timing for when it's appropriate to say or do something. I spend a lot of time considering scenarios before I make decisions. I'll usually go with a hunch, my intuition, what's the most likely cause. I do my best problem solving in my head away from whatever it is. I step back outside of things, think for a while, and make adjustments—could this be better than that, how do these react, and how does the whole system go together? I'm willing to do the upfront work, which makes it expedient because I never have to repeat it.

In my work, I don't want to be just doing stuff for the sake of doing stuff. I like to accomplish things—make a contribution. That's real important. I take a "do it" type of approach. It's very practical. It's very here and now. That does not mean I don't take into consideration the big picture and what's down the road and what's best for the organization, but at the same time my big focus is "let's get this show on the road and let's do it." I do it as well as I can. Then I think very well on my feet. I can be quick with the verbal comeback—I like the impact. I just get in there and do it, and whatever job I go into, I hit the ground running. And I'm very competitive, often with myself. I tie one hand behind my back and see if I can still do it.

Those times that I have to use my heart, it drives me crazy because I'm looking for things in clear-cut answers. I have a hard time agreeing that other people look at things completely differently. People should think things through. I have a problem with people reading between the lines. They hear words I never say, and I select my words carefully. I can take myself out of it so I usually don't take things personally. And I find I have to make a point to remember that people are part of the equation. I have to work that in.

I rarely work on one thing at a time. I get an idea and chase it down. I'm always studying—not just books but looking at what interests me. I customize everything I touch; people tell me I can't do something, and I say sure I can. And I like time to just sit down and enjoy. But when I have too much time I tend to just pick away at things. I am really much better when there is a deadline.

I look at the world as a place to enjoy. I like things to smell good, taste good, look and feel good. I love exploring the outdoors. The peace and stillness, the little noises and different views. I feel really comfortable out there. I have no desire to be with people when I don't know anybody. It's a delightful sensation when I see an animal.

I don't like the social stuff. It takes too much time, too much energy. I'm bored. I can't figure out how to make myself more relaxed, and I never really know what I'm supposed to be saying. I have only a few close friends that I really see a lot. Yet people have seen me as someone very lively and talkative. That's the part of me that likes life to be an adventure.

I like flexibility in what I do. Fun means something that interests me. Organized things don't come to me easily, but I can do them. I've always found ways to make things fun. It's a game to make sure you can come to the next point where you have freedom again There's something insincere about doing something just because of somebody or something else. What I do has to make sense, have impact. I cannot stand just busy work. It has to be meaningful. I have an incredible amount of enthusiasm and passion for certain things that I do and want to see done.

Motivator Presenter

TEMPERAMENT: ARTISAN
INTERACTION STYLE: GET THINGS GOING
PERSONALITY TYPE CODE: ESFP

SNAPSHOT

Theme is performance. Warm, charming, and witty. Want to impact and help others, to evoke their enjoyment, and to stimulate them to act. Want to make a difference and do something meaningful. Often masterful at showmanship, entertaining, motivating, and presenting. Thrive on social interaction, joyful living, and the challenge of the unknown. Like helping people get what they want and need, facilitating them to get results.

PORTRAIT

Themes

For Motivator Presenters, life is a process of stimulating action—getting things going to get things done—preferably having a variety of projects going at once. It is not enough to just have a feeling; it is important to act on that feeling. They accomplish an amazing amount, often juggling a wide range of projects—all with a sense of style. They have a talent for presenting things with a "look", with flair, and so others can more easily understand and use those things. They are the "natural actors" who meet what the environment gives them and engage others. They enjoy opening up people to all the possibilities they see. Instead of roadblocks and problems, they see challenges.

They have a healthy respect for freedom, theirs and others. Freedom is so important to them that anything that takes it away meets with strong resistance, even on small matters. Freedom from boredom gives them the strength to do what they need to but don't want to. For them, anything is possible as long as they have freedom! Taking what others view as risk is part of their daily life. They perceive a choice as risky only when it would limit their options and variety.

In their thought processes, they often experience a swirl of input all at once. To manage all these nearly simultaneous perceptions, they want to know what is relevant so they can focus their attention—what's the goal? Then they process the information so fast, they know what is important and what is wanted—they "get it." Then they want to be off, achieving the goal. They often find it frustrating to have to stay tuned in, while others are delving deeper or going methodically from A to Z.

Many aspects of life interest them and they have a love of learning. Their talent for displaying and presenting information gets people interested, excited, and involved.

Interpersonally, they are warm and friendly. People open up and relate easily to them. Others are often charmed by their genuine caring, willingness to help, and generosity. They are keen observers of others and very alert to nonverbal cues. They are responsive to those clues, often adapting to others' wishes to make their lives easier and happier. They want to give others the freedom they so value themselves.

Even though they have a talent for noticing and responding to nonverbal cues, they can place meaning on them that was not intended. When they misread others' intentions, they can find themselves trapped in a web of complexities.

Relationships

For Motivator Presenters, relationships are about caring, sharing experiences, and having fun together. They are quite generous with their time and possessions. They are great at asking the right questions or making an immediate suggestion and getting a genuine response. They make the effort to get involved, don't want to be left out of the loop, and often wind up being the center of attention. The upside is that in talking with people, they work really hard to see other people's points of view. They can be very accommodating until they feel taken advantage of. They have an enormous desire to help and they are sensitive to the pain and suffering of others.

In their close relationships, they like having fun, doing things together. They don't like dealing with relationship issues in an impersonal, abstract way but prefer relating personally. When there is deep caring, it's very important and they can be very loyal. If things are going poorly, they will try to make the best of things for quite a long time. But if the situation doesn't change, then they will want to stop sitting around and go out and start anew. They like affection and showing real feelings and visible gestures of caring.

SELF-PORTRAIT
From Conversations with Motivator Presenters

What's it like to be you?

I like variety. I like people. I am whatever is happening at the moment. I accomplish as much as I can to keep from getting bored—I find something I like and can tolerate, that I can see myself good at down the road. And I'm almost always up and positive. I always have a compliment and look for the good in a situation. I love the simple things in life, and I'm also interested in people and a lot of different things. I look at life's possibilities: the excitement of what might come out of a situation and what I might learn about a person and how I can help.

Freedom is the most important thing. If I don't have freedom, then what do I have?

I love talking to people. Making and having friends is gratifying, and I value my friendships. People see me as someone they can tell something to and not just as boring or average. Somehow I charm people, and I am very genuine in my interest. I observe the game of life, and a lot of times it's about being open and observant on my part. Whenever I find things getting heavy, I say something light to make everyone laugh again. I am offended when things are impersonal and harsh. Some people are so serious and many people feel guilty about having fun. Fun is important because I can get more work done in a few hours than most people do in a whole day. My biggest contribution is in just listening to what people are trying to do, probing and pushing and mirroring back to them what I hear they're saying.

I love not having to practice and still being good at something. I don't like having to do a lot of planning. I want to accomplish something and move on to the next thing. I am really good at pulling things off, especially if there is a last-minute crisis. It's just a matter of trying to keep things together, doing what you have to do in the moment. Being outside, getting physical, is also something I have a need for. Everyone always wants me on their team. People say I'm lucky.

I want to be of value. And I want there to be an equal exchange. I will give a lot but not so people use me—that limit is a very fine line. Sometimes I don't have a clue what the person needs, but given enough pieces I can help them solve their problems.

Don't let me sit down and have to do a repetitive task. I want to be efficient and fast. I'm able to simplify things and say whether it's going to work or not. I have fairly grounded views and can see things fairly quickly. I don't get mired down. I believe in moderation and balance. I only want to do something once, and any structure I put on is for a short time only, to be sure we're all heading in the same direction. People don't expect me to be organized, but I am.

I believe that if there's a problem, until somebody actually does something about it, then it's all just talk. It's not real. If there's no real progress, then eventually I'm out of there. I like people to know that they have a real place in the world, that they can do something, that they can actually physically act and that will make a difference. Everyone is unique and has a contribution to society, and maybe they don't have a plan, but I feel great when I can help someone realize they are special.

When the moment that I am living in becomes difficult, then I close up physically. I just move through life and react as things come up. I can get worried about the future and go down this long road of awful possibilities or thinking about the past, especially if others will be affected.

I am an individual. I can't imagine following others, and it's a waste of time if someone's not going to do their best. I want freedom for being able to do what I want to do when I want to do it. Don't tell me I can't do something. Rules and regulations infuriate me. Doing something by the book isn't always logical or reasonable. What makes a difference is if you do a good job or not. Do a good job and I respect you. I want to do my best.

Composer Producer

TEMPERAMENT: ARTISAN
INTERACTION STYLE: BEHIND THE SCENES
PERSONALITY TYPE CODE: ISFP

SNAPSHOT

Theme is composing, using whatever is at hand to get a harmonious, aesthetic result. Talents lie in combining, varying, and improvising, frequently in the arts but also in business and elsewhere. With their senses keenly tuned in they become totally absorbed in the action of the moment, finding just what fits the situation or the composition. Thrive on having the freedom to vary what they do until they get just the right effect. Take action to help others and demonstrate values. Kind and sensitive to the suffering of others.

PORTRAIT
Themes

For Composer Producers, life is a process of taking advantage of opportunities and being free to do so is like a dream come true. They somehow know how to stick with what's important and not sell out to the opportunities.

They seem to tap into what is extremely important to others and to themselves. They are the ones who listen to what others want and somehow pull together what is just right to get them just what they wanted, maybe even more than was expressed. It all looks so easy that others often underestimate what went into it. They have an amazing talent for creative problem solving and take a great deal of pleasure in helping people solve problems.

In their thought processes they are constantly composing. From their continual, random scanning of available resources, they find just the right idea, color, action, line, word, and so on to pull together a cohesive whole. Then they tinker with it until it feels like what is needed. They often get so absorbed in the creative moment, perfecting the piece, they can lose track of time.

They enjoy building relationships and attracting the loyalties of others while at the same time being their own true self. To not have their own personal style—to be boxed in and not be free to be however they see is needed in the moment—is worse than death to them. They will go to great lengths to avoid being pigeonholed and labeled. It is very important to them to play against the expectations others have of them, yet they often wind up exceeding those expectations when left to their own devices.

Interpersonally, their ability to build relationships can hide their intense need for privacy. And the challenge is always to balance freedom with connection.

They often struggle with nurturing their own self-esteem and sometimes needlessly beat up on themselves. Others may not even notice their struggle because their style is so quiet and unassuming.

Relationships

For Composer Producers, relationships are about camaraderie—having fun doing things together, interacting, and yet also being free. What's important is the sense of friendship, being able to say anything or say nothing and not have to think about or check what they're doing to get another's approval. Some things are just too deep for words. They judge someone on actions, and if others are good to them, then they're good in return. They trust people who aren't going to manipulate and hurt them. They can be very accommodating and agreeable, loyal and sympathetic. They need autonomy and will do what they can to accommodate others; feeling trapped may come suddenly. They want to do what they want to do and may see that as selfish of themselves. Yet they will follow through on a commitment, even though they wind up feeling trapped. They don't need to know that much about a person; being personal is not about self-disclosing but about helping. They listen to establish trust and then turn around and try to help the person. A big negative for them is when the other person never does anything with the help they offer. They are impatient with that.

In their close relationships, they are open to relationships but slow to commit. They commit if it's important to the other person and they get a feeling of a partnership. And then they are loyal, as long as they have some freedom. They don't like to constantly talk about the relationship; they assume if it's good today, then it will still be good tomorrow. Sometimes they feel like the other person just needs to give talking a rest and enjoy doing things together.

SELF-PORTRAIT
From Conversations with Composer Producers

What's it like to be you?

Probably I'm the happiest when things are just a little different everyday. I don't want to commit to any particular way to be. I want to be able to be a lot of ways. In my mind, I am peacefully assimilating myself to a lot of different situations, flowing easily between them all. Most people don't understand there's a lot going on inside. It's always different, and if it's not always different, it's no fun.

When I'm someplace, doing something, I'm really there. The whole experience is related to that time and place. And people only see the part of me that is with them that day. That's who I am for that day, but little do they know that tomorrow I might be different.

I'm reserved when I first meet people, but I am friendly, warm, and outgoing once I've gotten to know someone. I really enjoy listening to people, hearing other people's stories and learning about them. I remember a lot of the details. I ask a lot of questions and like the challenge of recognizing where people are coming from and why they might be coming from that perspective. I love the give and take of conversations. I really feel thrilled and excited learning from that intellectual energy combined with that emotional energy. It gives me a sense of the person. In any situation, I love the give and take, the playfulness and energy, the excitement and a little bit of competition, a little bit of one-upsmanship. But when it becomes abrasive and people personally attack others, I'm offended.

I have a lot of interests and I can get interested in one thing, and then something else comes along and that looks fascinating. I enjoy using the skills that I do have, and they're varied. I'm always on the lookout for something that uses my skills and abilities, that will give me variety and still be stimulating and let me have a mission with people. In my best jobs, I was connecting with people and problem solving and often using tools, adapting equipment or techniques.

My nature is when things get to a crunch, I'll make something happen that will make it all right. I just know that I can do that and will do that. I love solving people problems.

But part of me shivers if someone tells me their expectations of me, even if they're expectations I have for myself. I need the freedom to be able to change my mind or direction. I like to get a feel for what they're looking for and then just make it happen and hope they enjoy it. And don't ask me how I did it because I have a difficult time communicating that. It's whatever moves me at the time. I probably don't even remember half of what I've done. I can spin around doing nothing and then spend two minutes and get something done. It's a whole process that I can't communicate, because it's not something that can always be written down on paper—because when I'm doing it, I'm enjoying it. It's like I'm in a different world. It's not a task to me—it's a creative outlet.

I enjoy family and friends. I enjoy being with them and doing things with them—developing that relationship, bonding with them. I carry through with my commitments and I'm a very responsible person. Deep friendships are important to me, but not too many.

When I am angry I get quiet. Others don't know though, that's the problem. Because it's not an external, visible reaction—it's more passive, turned inward. I'm trying to think it through to figure a way to get my point across so they understand because I wouldn't want to attack somebody. That's something about me, that noncommunication, or withdrawal.

I like recognition. It's very important to get complimented soon after an accomplishment. If something goes unnoticed or unrewarded, it doesn't have the immediate impact that I want. I've been learning my own positive self-talk. I tend to be a workaholic at whatever it is I am doing. You might say I'm a perfectionist. I want people to be impressed with my performance. I don't want anyone to be unhappy with my performance so I continue to perform, and that is kind of a driving force. It has been a constant struggle to not overdo it. I need a positive environment to work in and I need the people I'm working with to support me.

Implementor Supervisor

TEMPERAMENT: GUARDIAN
INTERACTION STYLE: IN CHARGE
PERSONALITY TYPE CODE: ESTJ

SNAPSHOT

Theme is supervising, with an eye to the traditions and regulations of the group. Responsible, hardworking, and efficient. Interested in ensuring that standards are met, resources conserved, and consequences delivered. Talents lie in bringing order, structure, and completion. Want to keep order so the organization, group, family, or culture will be preserved. Thrive on organizing and following through with commitments and teaching others how to be successful.

PORTRAIT
Themes

For Implementor Supervisors, life is a process of educating themselves so they can be informed and learn the best way to do things. They have a talent for bringing order to chaotic situations by setting up routines, schedules and standard operating procedures. They want to have a sense of being in control of the situations they feel responsible for. They enjoy making sure everything runs smoothly. When they don't get to organize and complete projects, they are cut off from their main source of energy.

Their industrious, work-hard attitude helps them be accountable. They tend to work hard, but they believe it is important to balance work with play.

Having a philosophy of life provides the consistency they need in order to build a strong foundation. The steps to success are built on that foundation. Time is not to be wasted. Often, they so quickly see the right way to do tasks, others think they are being bossy and overbearing when, in reality, they may still be open to new ideas. They simply think, this is the best way for now. They show caring and concern less in their manner but more in being responsible and helping out.

Keeping up traditions with family, friends and institutions is important. Traditions provide a sense of belonging and membership as well as the predictability and continuity they crave. They carefully weigh risk and innovation against the likelihood of success. They seek to be well balanced and not weird in some way. They really do want to be liked and accepted. Their need to belong keeps them from straying too far from their cultural mainstream.

Their thought processes tend to be sequential and associational. They notice what is missing and out of order. They depend on a wealth of life experiences to help them recognize how what they are taught connects with the methods to make things happen. Once the association is made and compared, the new information, process, or tool is put to use right away.

They have a strong sense of quality and economy. They have a propensity for searching out the people, places, and things that meet their standards and are the most judicious investment. Then they often end up disappointed because whatever it was didn't turn out the way they thought it should.

Relationships

For Implementor Supervisors, relationships are about commitment. Relationships can also be about teaching people how to be responsible and what's important so others will be successful. They tend to have high expectations. The downside is their tendency to take charge, pushing and educating the other person on the right way to do things. They enjoy being with people, keeping track of everyone, and staying connected. They find it very satisfying to have people who will support and stand by them. They want stable relationships where they know they can count on the other person. Their relationships are built on a solid foundation of structure and routine. They tend to do a lot of taking care of what needs to be taken care of, working very hard, and giving of their time.

In their close relationships, they do like to have fun and even be silly. They have a sentimental side that is often hidden but shows in touching moments and a fondness for reminiscing over good times past. They are not expressive very often, especially of negative emotions, because they are so focused on the task at hand. Sometimes they are overly tactful to "be nice." They really don't want to hurt others and are likely to show their caring in what they do, the extra steps they take. They love an active social life.

SELF-PORTRAIT
From Conversations with Implementor Supervisors

What's it like to be you?

I like for things to be organized, and when they are not, I'm great at getting them organized.

I am very strong on work ethic and expect that from others. I cannot just sit around and do nothing for very long, especially if I have a lot to do and I don't have a plan. I am extremely organized when I work and I can work on four or five things through the course of the day. I think about what I have to do on the way to work or the way home or the night before. It's very gratifying to work extremely hard and sacrifice in order to take care of people, and I like when people appreciate that I have given of myself for them. I feel a lot of responsibility for what goes on when I have put time and effort into something and want to see that continue.

Things have to make sense to me. They have to be reasonable, logical, and simple and when they are not, that's frustrating. I think a lot of my life is tied up in responsibility and structure and organization. That's key—to have a frame around which to build everything else. It's satisfying to see something that was not working start working with tangible results. Once the structure is in place, then it fades into the background and allows the other, relational elements to bloom. You've got to have that backbone and structure or the rest of it falls apart. I can't relax when things aren't done right.

I have a sense of order and I like making sure things run smoothly, the practical nuts and bolts, on a day-to-day basis. Planning is challenging and exciting. I make sure others have what they need, not just what they want. I am pretty fast paced and want things done, and I get aggravated when people are late. I want to keep ahead of things to be ready to move on to the next thing. I am always trying to find the best way to save money, but I have very high expectations and I take the extra steps that need to be done. I take pride in my accuracy and detail, and I take pride in my accomplishments.

I have a very strong family commitment. I enjoy good neighbors and loyal friends. Values and traditions are important because I think a lot can be gained from those. And celebrating is fun. I think it's important to teach responsibility and encourage talent, shaping and molding and moving people in the right direction. Sharing my experiences in life is satisfying. I enjoy the simple things—walking, good food, looking at flowers, home life and my family. I love to put something together for fun to see what makes it tick.

I have always been very confident about the choices I make. I am fairly forward with how I think and I am not always particularly tactful. I have to think about how to be appropriate, to have some grace and empathy sometimes. But when I feel like I'm not in control, when someone is trying to take advantage of me, I very much let someone know about it. I'd prefer to research things very hard to make sure I'm not walking into something bad. Security is very important. I'm always trying to be efficient.

I'm not the type of person that can see a different future before it is actually there. I plan for the future by looking at the present facts. I see what's in front of me in the current situation and weigh the pros and cons of the alternatives. Until that happens, I don't really see all the coming changes in advance or how the future is affected. So I never really understand why people are doing the things they do. But once things happen, it's clear and my desired goals for the future are generally a driving force.

I hate when things fall apart because of disorganization and lack of leadership. I hate fraud, inefficiency and waste, cheating and stealing, lack of loyalty and integrity, and people who don't play by the rules or are only going after their own good. When people take the easy quick way out that really irritates me. And I resent it when other people don't respect my time. I need people I can depend on, and I get rid of people I can't depend on.

I have a lot of common sense. I believe you can build leadership by giving people genuine responsibility and genuine recognition, and I'm someone who can get things done. Sometimes people think I am too structured, but I feel best when I accomplish a lot. I relax when my work is done.

Planner Inspector

TEMPERAMENT: GUARDIAN
INTERACTION STYLE: CHART THE COURSE
PERSONALITY TYPE CODE: ISTJ

SNAPSHOT

Theme is planning and monitoring, ensuring predictable quality. Thorough, systematic, and careful. See discrepancies, omissions and pitfalls. Talents lie in administrating and regulating. Dependable, realistic, and sensible. Want to conserve the resources of the organization, group, family, or culture and persevere toward that goal. Thrive on planning ahead and being prepared. Like helping others through their roles as parent, supervisor, teammate, and community volunteer.

PORTRAIT

Themes

For Planner Inspectors, life is a process of drawing up plans and being prepared. Having things planned out gives them a measure of comfort and safety. Then they can be sure everything will be taken care of. They like to be orderly, systematic, and organized to be sure they don't overlook anything that should be done and to control for things that might go wrong.

They take responsibility for making sure the details of a task are completed to the agreed upon standards and on time. To not follow through on a commitment is nearly incomprehensible to them, and they go to great lengths to make sure whatever needs to be done will be accomplished. Their attitude is that you have to get your work done before you can really enjoy playing. Yet they do like to laugh and joke, even on the job—a side of them sometimes missed by others.

Being active in the community gives them another place besides work and home to be responsible and to contribute to the social structure that keeps society going. Take away their family, work, and community roles and you take away their sources of energy. They enjoy cultivating good qualities in themselves and in others.

They have a lot of loyalty to their roles and take them very seriously, sometimes putting up with conditions most people would avoid or escape. For them, showing they care by supporting one's family, being a good parent, a good worker, or even a good child is most important. One characteristic they are always respected for is doing the right thing. Somehow they manage to bear life's burdens and overcome adversity.

Their thought processes tend to be sequential and structured. First they line up the sequence of what is happening to see exactly what the problem is. They have a keen sense of past experiences to reference for constructing solutions, which they mentally test out for what is likely to happen and any negative effects. They are particularly talented at seeing the pieces of a project, what's missing, and how they go together.

When they reach the end of a task, they look back and often have a sense of "If only I had known then what I know now!" Learning so much in hindsight can be painful at times. They put the knowledge learned in their memory bank so they can apply it in future situations.

Relationships

For Planner Inspectors, relationships are about caring and responsibility. They enjoy giving of their time and experience and want to set a good example. They feel very responsible for those in their care. With a strong sense of honor, they feel it is their duty to keep the family unit, the work group, or the organization together and make sure everything is okay. They will work very hard as providers. The downside is that they can become so focused on their responsibilities to work that they neglect their responsibilities to be more personally involved. They are intensely loyal in all their relationships. Having stable relationships is important, and if educating the other person hasn't worked, they may overlook that person's irresponsibility in order to maintain stability. However, they can eventually get angry when others don't follow through and aren't pulling their weight.

In their close relationships, they are loyal and faithful. Traditional roles suit them well. They tend to hold in emotions and be less expressive. They can be very sentimental at times, especially over reminders of the past. Thoughtfulness and steadiness are the hallmarks of their relationships. They are more likely to give practical gifts than romantic ones. They need to make sure they get enough solitude, especially at the end of the day to review all that has happened and plan for the next day.

SELF-PORTRAIT
From Conversations with Planner Inspectors

What's it like to be you?

I think for the most part I try to make my life pretty structured, and one thing that other people can depend on is that I have a very strong sense of duty.

I'm a team player but I work best with some time alone. I like it when everything is laid out and I can just concentrate on doing the job. I hate it when I don't know where I am going, and I like feedback so I know I'm on the right track. If part of the job entails ambiguity, that's fine just as long as the goal is to reduce ambiguity. I like being financially secure with the bills paid on time so my family can enjoy the things that we like to do. I like to have a fallback plan. I do like to laugh and have fun too, but work is more important to me, and then I make my little jokes. I always think I have to get my work done before I can go out or go home, when I can just sit down and relax without anything hanging over my head. I take responsibility seriously, and if I'm going to put my name on something, my desire is to insure it's as good as it can be.

A sense of right and wrong is extremely important, and I will not just stand by and watch people doing things wrong. It really tears me apart. I tend to want things in order and people doing the right things. I want to have some rules. I always wanted to please people, and a safe environment to me is where I don't have to compete with anyone else's wishes. If I get into a situation where I feel very strongly and can't articulate the words or can't win, I just don't say anything. I tend to put up with conflict rather than deal with it. I try to deal with stress, but I am not necessarily a good confronter. I would like to be more of a stress avoider.

I find myself duty bound sometimes and find that I do things because of what's expected of me. People can trust and count on me, and I am very dependable, almost to a fault. I strive to keep balance between work and home, and if I'm going to provide for my family I'm going to have to swallow some things at work. When I see families that really want to be together, that's a

relationship that those people worked at for many years to achieve. Being a friend means caring enough about an individual to call them to see how they are doing, and if I can see someone has held true to their word, then they've probably gained my trust. If you were to ask me to define the word *love*, you would get responses like *caring*, *responsibility*, and *loyalty*.

I am a very private person and I don't like a lot of attention. Although I enjoy being with people, observing them, and just being a part of the group, I really like some solitude. People who don't know me perceive me as pretty formal and rigid, and then I'll get out of character and people don't know how to deal with that. They misinterpret my subtle sense of humor. I do have some ability to improvise every once in a while. I take a lot of pleasure in the simple things.

With a problem, I will try to look at all the parts and line them up to insure I don't miss something. I have to force myself to look at the big picture and solve it before I can say, "Yes, this is going to work." I'm not the idea person, but if I have experience I will give my opinion about how I think it should be done. If it's new, I am very much apt to sit back and take it all in and sit on it and think about it. I try to catch myself, but it's so unnatural for me to see the good side of things, and turning around my perspective takes a lot out of me. I want a rock-solid case for why I feel the way I do. A lot of my ideas are very practical, not theoretical—the down-to-earth stuff people really need to know. Sometimes when people don't see my point, I tend to withdraw or stand back.

I can't stand people who don't care for others, who are irresponsible or rude, who shoot their mouth off without knowing what they are talking about or who don't do what they are supposed to do and want something for nothing. I especially can't tolerate people who don't take other people's time or privacy into consideration.

I get up in the morning and do my routine. And I take time at the end of each day to try to plan what's happening the next day, what I'm going to be working on first, second, third, and so on through out the day, to eliminate the unexpected. Sometimes I might carry a book or something in case I have to wait somewhere. That makes life easy and full. Stability is important to me and change may not be that easy, but variety is good too. I seek advice when I need to change.

Facilitator Caretaker

TEMPERAMENT: GUARDIAN
INTERACTION STYLE: GET THINGS GOING
PERSONALITY TYPE CODE: ESFJ

SNAPSHOT

Theme is providing, ensuring that physical needs are met. Talents lie in supporting others and supplying them with what they need. Genuinely concerned about the welfare of others, making sure they are comfortable and involved. Use their sociability to nurture established institutions. Warm, considerate, thoughtful, friendly. Want to please and maintain harmonious relationships. Thrive on helping others and bringing people together.

PORTRAIT
Themes

For Facilitator Caretakers, life is a process of accepting and helping others. They enjoy friendly conversations where information—personal and professional—is exchanged to get to know people better. Managing people, at work or at home, is rewarding, even when difficult. They spend a lot of time hearing people out, voicing concerns, and accommodating needs. They genuinely admire the success of everyone and take great pride in the successes of their friends, family, and others in their circle. If they can help them along the way, giving them support and making things easier, they are truly satisfied. To not have contact with people and a sense of belonging is to be cut off from that which truly energizes them.

Their thought processes tend to be relational and sequential. They remember what's important for the family, the work group, and the community. It is as if they have a filing cabinet of all the specific details they've ever learned about the people they know so they can find that information easily to help others, to connect others, and to make them comfortable. The stories they tell about the people they know keep everybody in touch. This talent makes them the quintessential hosts.

In the interpersonal realm, they strive to keep life pleasant, often setting aside their own needs to provide for others and avoid conflict. This can become a problem when others don't give back some of the care and consideration given. Above all they want to maintain a sense of continuity in their relationships, their family, their business, or the community. Often that continuity is maintained by accounting for costs and protecting resources. Organizing, preparing, and remembering important events show they care just as much as the thoughtful acts they do. These also provide a sense of security and independence.

They are often disappointed by entrepreneurial projects. Sometimes in their desire to help others and be creative, they find themselves stuck doing a lot of hard work with not enough coming back to them.

Relationships

For Facilitator Caretakers, relationships are about doing things for each other—sharing a life and caring. Even business relationships are about sharing the life of a business, being a part of something, and creating a feeling of family. They like helping people build something in their lives, whether as friend, parent, or helpmate. Going the extra mile, sacrificing for what will benefit others, and understanding the other person are very important. Often they put the needs of the other person ahead of their own needs, and they can lose themselves to the relationship, often feeling somewhat used. They are very aware of hurting people's feelings and so may skirt heavy issues. They like listening and helping people with their problems and being very involved. If they have too many loyalties, they may give too much of themselves and stretch themselves too thin. They usually have lots of personal relationships and friends, enjoying lots of interaction.

In their close relationships, they tend toward the traditionally romantic yet spontaneous. Thoughtful gestures, time together, and mutual support are all important. They will have expectations about building something together, working toward a comfortable life, raising a family, or retirement. Sometimes it can be very difficult to get them to confront and move beyond bad relationships because they are so good at smoothing over conflict. They like a gregarious lifestyle and can be very supportive in extending hospitality and bringing people together.

SELF-PORTRAIT
From Conversations with Facilitator Caretakers

What's it like to be you?

I like to be involved and doing something. Much of my day is keeping contact with a lot of people. That's an important part of my life. I enjoy communicating with people, talking, going places and doing things, watching people and learning from watching. Bringing people together is a real pleasure. Sharing and time spent with friends and family, a special person, is very satisfying. I like to think about other people, and find I feel tremendous pleasure in reading them. When I see someone who just doesn't talk, sometimes I feel maybe they're missing something. I don't have trouble revealing what is very close to me, even with a complete stranger if I feel safe. Sharing confidences is a gift. I will anticipate others' needs.

A perfect day is feeling I've made a difference to someone. No tension, no conflicts, just something I've solved in a way that feels good to the best of the standards I've set for myself.

In my personal life, friends are important, and being a good friend and having good friends I can depend on makes life a pleasure and a joy. Long-lasting friendships or new ones—I generally care about others and they sense that. Maybe I care too much sometimes, but I want to listen to their background and rationale of why they did something. Part of me wants to tell them the answer right away, but sometimes people just want someone to listen. When I have a problem I bounce it off of people I respect and take into account how others involved will be affected. It can be difficult to take a hard line when people are going to be slighted, but sometimes I have to go through a lot of conflict, do what I must, and step on some toes. But I don't like conflict.

It's hard for me to be confrontational, even to the point where I can leave myself in a bad place because I really don't have the nerve to confront someone and say really what I think needs to be said. I tend to skirt the issue, put it off, because I am very aware of hurting people's feelings. But I am not afraid to face a challenge. I will stand up for the rights of others in spite of many obstacles because I believe in justice and helping people. Intolerance and prejudice, people who don't stand by their word or lie to cover up hurting someone else—these raise the hair on the back of my neck. It turns my stomach when people intentionally take advantage of and hurt others. It's not what the person says so much as how it's being said, to the point where I don't hear the message. I want to hear where the person is coming from.

Routine for me is actually something that can be comforting. I think the rhythm of it helps center me. I am good at organizing things. And you've got to have some fun out of your work in order to get up every morning and go. I like doing something just for fun, a random act of kindness. Appreciation and meaningful support can come in a variety of packages—when people intuitively know what I need or a hug or a day off. I've done a lot of the civic-type thing over the years in the community, volunteering part time. That's very rewarding. It's important to raise my kids to be good citizens, to be compassionate in their relationships, to work hard and stick with it through the hard times. Generally what goes around comes around if you wait long enough.

At times, even though by nature I want to be understanding, I can find myself torn between going by the rules and understanding. Often I'm frustrated with decisions because I'm caught between different values, and I have a reputation for expecting others to set goals for themselves and then try to obtain those goals. I tend to be a little too sensitive. I take criticism to heart. Please know that I may not respond right now but I heard you and I will respond.

I follow through on my commitments and obligations and believe in honest relationships and honest communication. I admire people who are not afraid to show affection, who are not embarrassed to try things even though they may not be good at them or are willing to make a change in their life, and who stand up for the rights of others and are not afraid to speak out when they feel someone is out of line. Personal growth means listening to myself and thinking about things, putting my priorities in order, and understanding that setbacks are only for today and that I can go on.

Protector Supporter

TEMPERAMENT: GUARDIAN
INTERACTION STYLE: BEHIND THE SCENES
PERSONALITY TYPE CODE: ISFJ

SNAPSHOT

Theme is protecting and caretaking, making sure their charges are safe from harm. Talents lie in making sure everything is taken care of so others can succeed and accomplish their goals. Desiring to serve individual needs, often work long hours. Quietly friendly, respectful, unassuming. Thrive on serving quietly without fanfare. Devoted to doing whatever is necessary to ensure shelter and safety, warning about pitfalls and dangers and supporting along the way.

PORTRAIT

Themes

For Protector Supporters, life is a process of noticing what's needed and what's valuable. They pay attention to what is important to each person and then put it all together to satisfy everyone. They know the ins and outs, what's customary and what's expected. Their familiarity with the way systems work makes providing order and structure natural for them to do. In this way, they provide support and help people. They give a tremendous amount of attention to detail and do a lot of preparing, organizing, and scheduling.

They like to feel a sense of accomplishment and that they've done a good job. They feel an obligation to get the work done. Their talent for careful and supportive organization is often taken for granted because it makes things run so smoothly that it is noticed only when it's not there. They often don't get the quiet recognition they need, but they continue to do the work anyway.

They enjoy traditions and the sense of belonging and security traditions provide. They like the comfort and predictability of knowing they can count on certain events or get-togethers. Without that sense of belonging

and security, they become quite anxious and worried. They also like to set things up ahead of time, to prepare and not rush into situations. That way they can work to protect the future.

Their thought processes tend to be sequential and relational. They have a keen sense of order and sequence. They have a way of listening and remembering all the little details and impressions about people. Then they compare new information to all of the memories they've stored away and relate it to the people they know and what they need.

People see them as being nice and agreeable. It is easy for them to be taken advantage of since they have such an unselfish willingness to volunteer, to help out in any way they can. They really care about the people in their lives and they like to be needed.

They are very respectful and dislike conflict. Sometimes they try to use the rules and organizational structure to get people to live together nicely and get along, and that can generate conflict.

Relationships

For Protector Supporters, relationships are about being supportive and caring. Conscientious, committed, and dedicated, they seem to be always willing to help. Warmhearted and sympathetic, they are always there and willing to help, to give people slack and time to figure things out. Being liked is important, and while they want to know what to do to improve, taking criticism is hard because they feel they've let the person down. They need acknowledgment from people they care about. They may have a hard time sticking up for themselves and need to learn to be assertive. They want to know what their role is. You can count on them when you need them. They establish a very personal connection and like to get to know people well. They are not usually open and talkative until they get to know someone.

In their close relationships, they are helpmates. Frequently taking the supporting role, they can become dependent and deferential. They like relationships set and secure, taking the time to get to know a lot about the other person. Gestures of kindness and thoughtfulness are important to them. As involved as they like to be, they need alone time, especially at the end of the day to review what has happened.

SELF-PORTRAIT
From Conversations with Protector Supporters

> What's it like to be you?

I like feeling I have helped someone with a concern, helping them figure out, deal with, and resolve the problem, knowing that what I recommended or advised really did help that person.

I am fairly quiet with an easygoing attitude and am modest to some extent. I do not mind being alone, although I do like to be with people too. I like having friends, and family is the most important thing in my life. I am a reluctant leader—I like to have some say in things and I am glad I am doing it, but if things go well with someone else as leader, then that doesn't bother me. Privacy is important, though it's nice to be thought of well by others. I like to have some independence; to be able to come and go as I please is nice.

I am dependable and conscientious. I have a big sense of obligation with work. Doing a good job is really important to me. Give me specifics and a plan on how you want me to do it. Brainstorming is generally harder—it's a skill to acquire. I prefer to work by myself without distractions because I like things done a certain way. It's taken me a while to learn that my work is much better quality when I'm drawing from those who see things differently. They help keep up my enthusiasm. And I get upset when work backs up—and it probably takes me longer than most people to do something because I am so thorough. But when I have learned a lot about what I do, I think I get the job done much faster and I can make difficult work look easy. I cannot stand people not doing their best job. I do what I say I'm going to do and stick with it until it's done. And I can find myself overcommitted. It's important to me to be able to say "Okay, this is enough responsibility for now, I don't have to climb that ladder at any cost."

Organization has always been a real strength. I do it all internally, in my head. I am fairly detail oriented and a very structured person. I have to have things in a certain place, with a plan and things prioritized, so I can leave things and pick up the next day where I left off. Being structured is a natural thing with me, to want to have things set.

I dislike conflict. I really care about treating people with a lot of respect. It's an emotional drain when I have to deal with different opinions and reconcile everyone. I give an opinion based on what I think is fair and what's been done in the past. What's decided for one person shouldn't be really any different than for another. I respect that people are certainly entitled to feel the way they feel, but in working or living together, decisions have to be made and things have to go a certain way. I need positive feedback that I'm doing a good job and that my opinions are similar to the opinions of others, to hear, "Yes, I think that same thing." I worry when there's disagreement. I question myself. I've learned to challenge what I don't feel is right, especially if someone does something to me that I don't feel I would have done to that person.

Anything really major in life can take forever to decide. I look to what matters to people, talk to them and get their ideas, then put it all together into something that satisfies everyone. I am more comfortable preparing first and then starting something, after I've pictured it in my mind, rehearsed it, and perfected it. I feel I do a good job expressing myself when I have a chance to prepare, although I do better in reflection. Answering questions on the spur of the moment can be hard too. I will take something minor and get all freaked out when it's nothing to get upset about. I'm very methodical and prefer things to be laid out. If it's a problem with me and another person, I can analyze the situation endlessly until I talk to the person again and straighten it out.

I consider myself adaptable to anyone. I feel that a lot of people think I am a nice person, and because I was always there for them in the past and willing to help, they try to take advantage of me. But as long as you are doing something okay with your life, then you are okay with me.

I need acknowledgment from people who I really care about. Compliments can be embarrassing face to face, though. A paycheck is nice recognition too. I like a day when everything works really well, when I get a lot done, people respond very positively and there is a lot of laughter. I have an unusual sense of humor, and I like laughter.

Strategist Mobilizer

TEMPERAMENT: RATIONAL
INTERACTION STYLE: IN CHARGE
PERSONALITY TYPE CODE: ENTJ

SNAPSHOT

Theme is directing and mobilizing. Talents lie in developing policy, establishing plans, coordinating and sequencing events, and implementing strategy. Excel at directing others in reaching the goals dictated by their strong vision of the organization. Thrive on marshaling forces to get plans into action. Natural organization builders and almost always find themselves taking charge in ineffective situations. They enjoy creating efficiently structured systems and setting priorities to achieve goals.

PORTRAIT
Themes

For Strategist Mobilizers, life is a process of leading—being the kind of leaders who maximize results by utilizing and developing the talents of those they lead. They enjoy forging partnerships to accomplish complex projects and strategically coordinate it all. They mobilize all the resources—people as well as financial and institutional—to achieve what they envision. To not have an opportunity to marshal these resources toward progress is to be cut off from what is truly energizing. Mentoring and empowering are more important than merely directing the actions of others for they are focused on the long term and don't want to have to direct everything all the time.

Their thought processes tend to be integrative and analytical. They easily integrate the insights they have from their intuitive explorations into a coordinated plan that sequences events in the most effective way. They tend to take their predictive creativity for granted as they effortlessly lay out a plan. What people notice most is how quickly they analyze and prioritize.

In the interpersonal arena, they balance peace and conflict—confronting important issues as they arise yet not letting unimportant ones disrupt the progress toward the goal. Others sometimes see them as brusque and critical and can miss the ways they show how much they care. Caring is shown less through gestures of kindness and affection than through personal action—doing things for people they care about and persistently pursuing goals and advice based on strategic thinking.

It sometimes seems to them they'll never get total control of managing all the details of time and resources. This feeling of inadequacy is one of the few things that can overwhelm them, even though they have a talent for coordinating multiple projects and completing tasks by their deadlines.

Relationships

For Strategist Mobilizers, relationships are about mutual problem solving and usually have a purpose—family, social, professional, or even mentoring. They have a tremendous desire for relationships to be positive and productive, often viewing them as yet another project to be coordinated. Competition geared toward mastery often becomes a part of their relationships, especially professional ones. They want to learn what the other person knows. They tend to be very honest in relationships—refreshingly honest for many people, harshly honest for others. And their honest opinions are often quite accurate! They like people who are going to make them smarter, who will make them push themselves more or learn more, and seek close association with people if that value is there. Usually not very self-disclosing, they will open up quickly and matter of factly with people they like and judge as friendly. Even then, they tend to keep their distance and may be hard to get to know on a personal level. They are often quick to judge when others seem stupid or do not take responsibility for their own actions.

In their close relationships, they prefer mutually autonomous relationships and may just go along with common social roles much of the time. They have a tendency to focus on their careers for that is where they get to exercise their talents the most and get the most gratification. The downside is that personal relationships often can be "put on the back burner" or a partner seen as an adjunct to their careers. When they realize the importance of the relationship, however, they put a lot of effort into staying connected, and they can be quite sentimental at times. Sharing activities, coaching, and mentoring are often an important part of the relationship.

SELF-PORTRAIT
From Conversations with Strategist Mobilizers

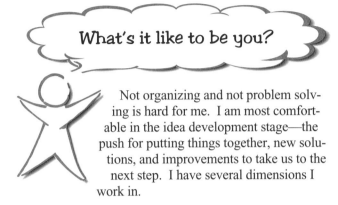

What's it like to be you?

Not organizing and not problem solving is hard for me. I am most comfortable in the idea development stage—the push for putting things together, new solutions, and improvements to take us to the next step. I have several dimensions I work in.

My focus has always been on finding what's preventing us from doing what we need to do. If it's lack of confidence or motivation, the solution is building that. If it's lack of skills, it's building skills. If it's rules or other inhibitors, I work to eliminate those. I value people, but I am quick to judge their value to the system and quick to judge my personal desire to be involved with them. I stand off if they don't meet my standards quickly, which can make me hard to know, and I think I am unwilling to get into other people's motivations.

My response to making a mistake is, "Did you learn anything? If so, great, it was worth it, and don't make the same mistake again." This kind of critiquing is easy for me, and I admire—and like to have around me—people who have a real, genuine concern for others and who see the positives. But then there is a time when I sit back and say people have to get on board with the way I see things because it's the right way to go. It took me a while to learn the value of cutting people some slack. Although I appear to dominate, when people get to know me, I really don't. I let them do their own thing. With people I judge as friendly or want to get to know, I open up quickly, although I don't actually go out and do things to make others like me.

I respect wisdom and kindness and competent, knowledgeable people who are willing to share with others. I won't buy into anything just because the person who says it is the leader. It has to make sense to me—consistent and free of contradictions. If it's a plan, I have to believe it's doable. If it's a philosophy, it must match mine from the outset. I think integrity means keeping one's word and sticking to my espoused principles even when it's easier not to. Honesty is important.

I really value progress, learning, and knowledge and have an intense need to know things. Probably this is where I get myself into a lot of projects because it is the opportunity to try something new. I tend to over research, and I have an innate ability to handle a great number of diverse things almost simultaneously. I can watch TV and finish a project and read a magazine all at the same time. I think I don't know how to relax. I can sit down and actually go through and identify the problem and gather alternatives and do a mental brainstorm by myself to come up with different alternatives. I force myself to see if I am not looking at something disjointedly or parochially before I come to a conclusion. And I try to look at the small things in order to look at the big picture, just using plain logic and connecting the dots to prognosticate what the likely outcomes are. Often the first conclusion was the right one anyway.

I actually believe you can do anything if you set your mind to it and are willing to pay the price. I will ask myself if I am willing to pay the price.

I tend to push to get the job done, sometimes without regard to others' feelings, and I hate repeating myself. Listening is a problem for me because I have probably already thought out things thoroughly, done my homework, and reached an answer before I even get to the stage of presenting it to other people. Similarly, I may get upset with others' behavior, but it is almost never personalized, which can be a drawback because then I haven't considered what caused the behavior and if I should make some kind of reconciliation.

I am my own worst critic. I want perfect achievement of myself, and sometimes I have a fear of suddenly waking up and being known as someone who doesn't really know anything.

I love to discover new approaches and really prefer creating and beginning things, organizing projects and programs, and then teaching someone else how to do them and handing them off. Although if someone has a better idea, then let's go with it, and if the system's values and mechanisms line up for me, whoever the leader is, then I guess I am probably one of the most loyal. Probably my goals are patience, wisdom, and discipline—wisdom to focus on the right priorities and correct decisions and patience to take the time to listen.

Conceptualizer Director

TEMPERAMENT: RATIONAL
INTERACTION STYLE: CHART THE COURSE
PERSONALITY TYPE CODE: INTJ

SNAPSHOT

Theme is strategizing, envisioning, and masterminding. Talents lie in defining goals, creating detailed plans, and outlining contingencies. Devise strategy, give structure, establish complex plans to reach distant goals dictated by a strong vision of what is needed in the long run. Thrive on putting theories to work and are open to any and all ideas that can be integrated into the complex systems they seek to understand. Drive themselves hard to master what is needed to make progress toward goals.

PORTRAIT

Themes

For Conceptualizer Directors, life is a process of maximizing achievement—not just accomplishments—but achievements that reflect penetrating thought and insightful integration of all they've learned. And they can never learn enough. A constant drive for self-mastery is what keeps them focused on achievement, whether masterminding a project or venture or developing their social or physical skills. They enjoy mastering anything that attracts—the more challenging, the better.

Their thought processes tend to be integrative, analytical, and often complex. It is as if they see a map of a domain by analyzing what is really there and then build a vision of where to go that no one has ever thought of yet. Then the long-range strategizing just happens. This internal map keeps the vision in focus, and they just know the action steps that need to be planned for and taken. Sometimes they dress the plan up with logic because all others see is the plan, not the underlying concepts behind it.

Systems thinking comes naturally to them as they quickly grasp the interrelatedness of everything in their universe. They have a talent for seeing the reasons behind things. People often don't appreciate the complexity of thought behind what is a deceptively simple strategy that keeps them and their endeavors on the leading edge.

It is important for them to maintain independence, to be an independent thinker. In the interpersonal realm, this can become a problem as people misread the independence and masterminding for arrogance rather than an inner desire to find useful solutions that will help people in the long run. They know how important it is to get to where they (we) are going and must hold fast to the vision even if others don't see it. Realizing progress toward goals is necessary for their survival. When progress is not being made, life is dull and draining. Yet progress often feels illusive, since it may be outside their control. In response, they develop strategies like recruiting others who share their vision.

Interacting with others is perhaps their biggest challenge as they apply their strategic thinking to the social arena. Finding ways to be spontaneously genuine requires them to set aside strategy and independence, which is sometimes more difficult than mastering social skills.

Relationships

For Conceptualizer Directors, relationships are about progress and should serve a positive purpose. Even occasional growth will be enough to continue a relationship, but if there is no improvement they will give up because there is apparently no point. They will want to learn from the experience and then go on. They enjoy collegial relationships with others who stimulate their thinking. They can be either stubborn about their own point of view or in a state of complete doubt about what's going on. They are often oblivious to the effect of their responses on others and can be defensive if feeling questioned. They tend to be absorbed in work yet enjoy time with people, but they tend to see purely social time as wasteful. They can instantly latch onto someone they have a strong intuition about and will feel very loyal to that person, staying for the long haul. Staying means the relationship is not a waste of time; it fits in the larger scheme of life.

In their close relationships, they want an ultimate connective experience. They are very private, showing affection only to those close to them. They don't like the feeling of being indecisive and kept up in the air emotionally. Because communicating emotions feels embarrassing, they want some structured way to interact and communicate, to leave no room for uncertainty. This can make them look more traditional than they really are.

SELF-PORTRAIT
From Conversations with Conceptualizer Directors

What's it like to be you?

I often feel I am missing something, that I have a perspective or viewpoint that isn't widely shared and that I am decades ahead of my time, maybe more. It's like being caught in a time warp.

I tend to be someone who looks at all the what-ifs, thinking way ahead with a vision of things and anticipating. I'm always interested in extending myself into areas I don't do well in. I'm a good problem solver from that perspective. I like to go through anything I can think of before I act—the implications, what others have tried before and their effect, my options and their consequences, who to mobilize and in what time frame. I like coming up with new ideas about how to approach a situation until I find a solution that feels right. And I like to think that solution will be something that works for everyone. I experience problems as challenges, not as things that can't be dealt with or accomplished. Challenges can always be dealt with

I am naturally organized, structured, and analytical. If a project enters my mind it immediately assumes the form of its pieces, its basic structure, and what order— first, next, last—it will take to get it done. This isn't something I do, it happens instantaneously without effort. Issues are multifaceted and I try to think from different perspectives, not only my perspectives but others' too. And I've found it's good to gather as many facts as I can. Sometimes there is a piece that needs to be thrown out, or maybe it's the seed of another project.

I won't do something if I feel I can't do it well. I prefer trying something, then critique after the fact. I will integrate the experience and never make the same mistakes again. I am satisfied when things work well, and I like to improve people's lives by reorganizing and introducing things in an understandable way that is explicit and clear and makes sense. Then someone else can come in and take over. I set very high standards for myself, and I believe it is possible to be competent at anything and everything I set my mind to.

I keep myself very private; that's a part of who I am. I keep people at arm's length. They have to gain my trust and interest. People are curious about me, I think, but only the brave try to figure me out. I feel very serious, but some I meet I just like a lot, and I can be spontaneously playful. I have a sensitivity to people and can feel warm with them, although many perceive me as intimidating, aloof or annoyed, or incredibly calm and competent about everything. People say I ask them good questions, not to make the decision for them, but to help them think through things. I look for systems that will make things better, and I am very much a person who seeks fairness and equality. People are very important, and I want to help them develop the skills they need to get on in life, whatever that means for each one of them.

There's always something to occupy my mind or attention. I must be using my mind in a purposefully creative way, pushing the envelope with the most creatively challenging thing I can do, being the originator of a solution to a problem that doesn't exist yet. It's a complex world, and I believe we each should develop as complex an inner life as possible with the facility to react or initiate in a wide variety of ways. The more successful one is at actively developing all of that and having access to that, the better things can be. If something really interests me I have an incredible ability to stick with it—even though I have a larger perspective, I can be very focused and zero in on a point. I have always seen the world at many levels.

Autonomy is important, to be respected for my own thoughts and feelings, ideas and creativity. I am turned off when people try to discredit my ideas or don't listen before they even understand, or when people don't try to do the best they can or fight against progress. And if the emotional piece is not well managed in my life, or not compartmentalized, work is very difficult. Chitchat is tedious. I don't know what to say, and I figure the other person isn't actually interested in me anyway.

Over time I have built a world-view, like constructing a map of the cosmos, and from this, essentially everything is understandable and anything is possible. All the things I've done, have been self-taught by picking up on or asking myself good, clear, penetrating questions to expose and articulate the hidden structures that underlie the experience of living.

Explorer Inventor

TEMPERAMENT: RATIONAL
INTERACTION STYLE: GET THINGS GOING
PERSONALITY TYPE CODE: ENTP

SNAPSHOT

Theme is inventing, finding ingenious solutions to people and technical problems. Talents lie in developing ideas into functional and innovative applications that are the first of their kind. Thrive on finding new ways to use theories to make systems more efficient and people better off. Hunger for new projects. Have faith in their ability to instantly come up with new approaches that will work. Engineers of human relationships and systems as well as in the more scientific and technological domains.

PORTRAIT

Themes

For Explorer Inventors, life is a process of being inventive, finding new ways to conceptualize problems. They want to find ingenious solutions that really resolve problems, not just fix them. They see the world through many lenses, from multiple perspectives using multiple models. They enjoy the creative process. New ideas and really creative, unusual, and efficient solutions often flood their awareness. Many of these ideas are way ahead of the times, and Explorer Inventors trust their instincts to strategically formulate success to get there. They are talented at building prototypes and launching projects. To not be able to share their insights about life's possibilities is a real energy drain. It is even worse to not have the ability to achieve success with those ideas.

In the interpersonal realm they have a way of trying to be diplomatic, of understanding where people are coming from. They like to be original in a way that everybody can use or benefit from. Ever the inviting host, they bring people together, wanting them to be at ease and to stimulate interesting conversations. They love the drama of the give and take, the lively debate, the vicissitudes of life.

Their thought processes tend to be abstractly random, often with very little concrete data seeking. They quickly conceptualize and hypothesize potentialities that are seemingly unrelated to the facts at hand yet turn out to be extremely relevant. They seek to understand the principles that underlie a process, seeing patterns and connections to the principles so quickly that others might think they've "made up" the answer, yet more often than not, that answer is right. The drive for understanding leads to a pattern of lifelong learning, both formally and informally.

They readily apply their talent for using a meta-strategy (strategy about strategy) to solve problems and to reach goals in their relationships—personal and professional. They are often surprised when strategizing relationships becomes problematic. Others haven't agreed to the problem-solving role and are just seeking to relate and often don't recognize and appreciate the good intentions of the Explorer Inventor.

Relationships

For Explorer Inventors, relationships are about generating and sharing ideas, interest, and activities. There is usually an easy first connection, and many love to travel all over, meeting new people and new cultures. They need to know the history and turning points of a person's life to really get to know someone. Stories and memories of past experiences make them feel connected. Since their relationships often revolve around a sharing of ideas, at some point they may wind up feeling inadequate or even stupid. If they are not feeling confident at that time, they may jump to critiquing the relationship. Sometimes mutual sharing can become competitive and not as fun for the other person. On the plus side, they are good at connecting with people and aligning with them, getting to know them and being a catalyst, seeing a lot of potentials in other people's activities, often more than those people can see.

In their close relationships, they often do a lot of problem solving, centering around creativity and imagination. They are very entrepreneurial, even in relationships, and may feel underappreciated for their brilliance. They judge the relationship by the way they experience the other person. They may have intense feelings inside but have a hard time expressing their emotions. They often think they've conveyed their emotions, but in reality, the partner remains in the dark about how they really feel. They tend to be very partner oriented, helpful, and supportive.

SELF-PORTRAIT
From Conversations with Explorer Inventors

What's it like to be you?

Life feels like a constant state of moving from one interesting thing to another, and I can get frustrated when there isn't enough time to pursue all those interesting things.

I have a wide range of interests. I love to explore the world, how other people live, what they believe in, and what their lives are like. I have a deep need to understand the human condition and what brings people to life, even above difficult odds. I like it when the conversation goes wherever it wants to go—deep imaginative, intellectual, or philosophical conversation. Going off on one theory or another is fun, but long stories with nothing to learn frustrate me.

Ideas mean change. When I meet people who have interesting ideas, talents, or projects, I want to get to know them and help them make whatever they want to do possibly much bigger, more successful, or more impactful than they had intended. I start aligning with them and building trust because I want to get invited in—to probably change whatever they want to do because I tend to see more possibilities. Then we cook up the project. It's fun to learn. I enjoy that in-the-moment experience of connecting things in my mind. Challenge and intellectual stimulation get me excited.

I just see a different world than the one in which I live, and I admire people who have genuine compassion and a commitment to serve others. I really respect people who have the ability to take the slings and arrows that come with leadership roles and working for change, who can cope with all the misunderstanding and resistance, who can say, "This is an idea whose time has come and we're going to get it done." It's important to me to be in a setting where people are committed, where facts are respected, and where there is a space for people to tell the truth or at least look for the truth—and be open to listening.

Colleagues describe me as someone they can go to when they want an idea or help with an issue or problem they're trying to solve. I often can condense or simplify a complex idea. I really often know the right words to use, not necessarily the right empathetic words but the right words. Coaching and giving ideas I do well. Just giving direction is boring. I don't feel things have to be done my way, but they have to be done well.

I am very partner oriented, and being creative together is what makes a relationship alive.

I work a lot, always looking for new projects, something to sink my teeth into, and I am constantly challenging myself to make things better. Things I've already figured out I like to put together in a format or structure, so I don't have to sit down and go through all the nitty-gritty details. I think in terms of the future—why am I here, what is this connected to, where are things going, where did they come from and wouldn't it be better if…? When my intuition is working it produces a lot of excitement and ideas.

I tend to look at things from a very objective basis. Sometimes I don't take the time to stop and thank people and let them know I'm trying to build on what they have already done. When I look at things, I am trying to figure out the system—looking beneath, behind, or above, somehow looking beyond the sensory data to figure out how it all works. I spend a lot of time trying to figure out in my head everything around me. Competence is a must, trying to perfect things, finding a new way. I am hardest on myself, with incredibly high standards, and I hold others to my standards even though sometimes I wish I hadn't. And yet I often seem pretty easygoing.

Fairness and consistency are really important. I feel that people should be treated with respect at all times, and I don't like behavior demeaning to others. When there is conflict I feel a compulsion to figure it out, to resolve it. When I'm personally involved, it can be difficult to initiate a discussion about the conflict. Sometimes I feel inadequate.

I think life is a puzzle and we keep playing with how to fit the pieces together. Something new and challenging is always more interesting to me than something I am already competent at.

Designer Theorizer

TEMPERAMENT: RATIONAL
INTERACTION STYLE: BEHIND THE SCENES
PERSONALITY TYPE CODE: INTP

SNAPSHOT

Theme is designing and configuring. Talents lie in grasping the underlying principles of something and defining its essential qualities. Seek to define precisely and bring coherence to systems based on the pattern of organization that is naturally there. Easily notice inconsistencies. Enjoy elegant theories and models for their own sake and for use in solving technical and human problems. Interested in theorizing, analyzing, and learning. Thrive on exploring, understanding, and explaining how the world works.

PORTRAIT

Themes

For Designer Theorizers, life is a process of becoming an expert. And they almost never feel quite expert enough. They enjoy reflecting on how things work, why they work that way, and what makes them not work and then really solving a problem, not just fixing it for now. They also enjoy generating ideas and seeing new patterns and elegant connections. These new connections activate their talent for design and continual redesign. The clarity they bring to defining problems as well as words helps them go straight to the essence of a problem, a situation, or a concept.

Their thought processes seem random, yet they are logically coherent. It is as if they hold a matrix in their minds with multiple connections, and their conceptualization and design work often involves crossing the arbitrary boundaries of thought and disciplines to activate the imagination and picture the patterns. Making discoveries is a better form of nourishment than food, for without these, their intellect would starve. These are the people who reflect on the process of thinking itself and seek to produce an elegant design to solve social as well as technical problems. Flashes of insight truly energize them.

In the interpersonal realm, they also engineer connections—connecting people with new ideas and information and sometimes with others. For being such basically solitary people, they have a surprising ability to network people with people, usually around expertise. They know who knows what and how well.

Their most satisfying relationships often come from sharing knowledge. Even then, they frequently detach to analyze a situation or problem before re-engaging. Others often misread this detachment as not caring, when often the analysis and problem solving are done on behalf of the other person.

They often say they struggle with attending to the physical world—like filing papers, dealing with repairs, deciding what to wear, or maintaining their own bodies. Even more, finding the right words to use to convey their clarity of thought often eludes them.

Relationships

For Designer Theorizers, relationships are a lot about expertise. They enjoy having a joint area of interest and expertise to share. They often seek out relationships to have different thoughts and experiences. Disruption that comes with conflict and strong emotion keeps them from thinking clearly, so they avoid confrontation unless it is necessary. Frequently they may find themselves lacking the interpersonal skills they need, and relationships can become competitive. Their penchant for precisely defining words, clarifying ideas, and pointing out inconsistencies can be wearing at times even if it is in the best interest of the other person, the group, or the project. A calm, conflict-free environment is preferred, and consultative relationships are preferred over hierarchical ones.

In their close relationships, they need autonomy, with the perspective that nobody has the right to "let" them do or not do anything. The notion that there is a role they are supposed to serve can be a surprise and a shock, and a relationship can feel like bondage if too many traditional roles are imposed. Traditional roles can interfere with their intellectual needs. The challenge for them in a relationship is to not be robotic and preoccupied with constant analysis and work or hobby interests. They may self-sacrifice for the relationship, sticking with one person in spite of difficulties. They can be very supportive about giving each other independence and going the extra mile to support that independence.

SELF-PORTRAIT

From Conversations with Designer Theorizers

What's it like to be you?

I want to know the truth and get down to the bottom of things. It's an internal life, living in the head, theorizing constantly about how things work.

I can link many thoughts and shoot off in multiple directions at once in an attempt to clarify and explain things really well or to try to represent the fullness of who I am and all the different things I can do and can't do. I like to design—not just implementation but the stuff before that. There is a goal, a theme, and I start from that and work through the specifics one by one, keeping the whole thing integrated as I go, until I come up with "the elegant solution." Often when I talk to people they only get from me a few steps—one, thirteen, a hundred. That's all that gets verbalized, and what's very clear to me either I've forgotten or find unnecessary to say out loud, which can come across as confusing at times.

I am very knowledge and big picture oriented. I want to bring everything that can be known into understanding a problem or situation. I enjoy working with those who think like I do but verbalize better. We can end up leaping forward rapidly and building off of ideas, asking questions with an answer in mind but wanting to verify things and learn more. If I am knowledgeable in that area, I always have something to add, to help better understand the idea and add something new. Although sometimes, even when I know we agree, people feel like I am trying to challenge them, which is frustrating because I am just doing it out of excitement. I try to understand all the variables and possible influences and then apply as broad a range of information as I can bring to the problem, to impact why the problem exists. I am interested in developing new skills and trying new ideas with those skills, and I am a good team member, and yet sometimes a little group work can go a long way. Most of all, I love to learn.

Central for me is honesty and integrity, especially intellectual integrity. If it's not an honest approach to the issue at hand or to the relationship or organization, then it becomes an illusion—it only appears to have substance. I respect people who are genuine, honest, and open and doing what they are good at and what they enjoy and are up front about what is important to them.

I have a penchant for clarity. Some people say I'm hairsplitting, but there is value in precision.

I don't like sloppy thinking, waste, and redundancy, and I am uncomfortable with sending out something that isn't as good as it can be, but it has to go out anyway. I like things thought through. Incompetence just sets me right off. I have very little tolerance or patience, especially if the person is above me or isn't really trying. I don't think I push people any harder than I push myself and most people probably push less, which is where conflict comes in. Some people say my standard may be way out of whack and I assume the other person is competent. I like to avoid conflict at all possible costs, but if it reaches a point where I can't go anywhere unless this gets resolved, then I will jump in and take care of it. That takes me a long time and I will go miles out my way to avoid that. It's an ongoing decision between fairness and not letting people walk all over me.

There is this constant balancing act between self-confidence and questioning myself. Sometimes I feel secure and comfortable about knowing and thinking about and recognizing a lot and knowing how to learn new skills and ideas and concepts. But I have an almost instant ability to detect limitations—not knowing enough, picking out what's missing, adding in an always-present feeling that it's not quite right, and not knowing everything there is to know with insufficient time to learn everything that is important.

I can be seen as too unfeeling, too quick to start into work with not enough basis laid out for the day, and I'm not much for the personal amenities or socializing. Yet it is important that others are aware they are important to me. It's not the first thing, but it's in my awareness. I tend to try solving personal problems all by myself. Then sometimes I wind up without accurate information from others or about how it will affect others. I believe there must be an answer or a solution if I can just figure it out.

Envisioner Mentor

TEMPERAMENT: IDEALIST
INTERACTION STYLE: IN CHARGE
PERSONALITY TYPE CODE: ENFJ

SNAPSHOT

Theme is mentoring, leading people to achieve their potential and become more of who they are. Talents lie in empathizing with profound interpersonal insight and in influencing others to learn, grow, and develop. Lead using their exceptional communication skills, enthusiasm, and warmth to gain cooperation toward meeting the ideals they hold for the individual or the organization. Catalysts who draw out the best in others. Thrive on empathic connections. Frequently called on to help others with personal problems.

PORTRAIT
Themes

For Envisioner Mentors, life is a process of succeeding at relationships. There can never be enough truly empathic relationships to foster mutual growth. They enjoy the creative process in many forms and often bring a fresh view to projects they enthusiastically work on. Realizing dreams—their own and others'— is what life is all about. To not have dreams to manifest and a chance to communicate and share values is to live a life with no meaning and no purpose, a fate worse than death.

For them, all of life is about the interpersonal, and they constantly seek opportunities to grow together through relationships. There are times when they value logical explanations. Having realizations that foster development and help them understand why the world is the way it is helps them lead a purposeful life. Learning from relationships is important and occasionally painful.

Their thought processes tend to be integrative and global as they seek to find ways to help others know themselves and their life's mission. Heeding the call to a life work or mission is tremendously important to them, and they are readily available to others to help

reveal to them their unique purpose. Sometimes they find themselves knowing what they do not want to know, yet to shut off their empathic knowing is to shut off a vital life force.

In the interpersonal realm, they often find that their ease in connecting with others becomes a hindrance to their own well-being as they get lost in the relationship and lose sight of their own identity until they learn to set boundaries. They often use their intuitive intellect to reconcile the past and the future as they seek to understand the meaning and significance of life events.

With such a talent for seeing potential in others and a focus on realizing that potential, they often find living in the present difficult. By the time an event happens, they have already lived it.

Relationships

For Envisioner Mentors, relationships are about connecting. Life is all about relating empathically, and people need lots of attention and commitment. Nurturing relationships is what they live for. There must be a sense of connection, to feel known, understood, needed, reassured, and praised. They often find themselves acting informally as counselors, even if that is not their profession. And that fulfills their daily dose of connection. The downside is they can become overburdened with others' problems. They invest a lot in all their relationships, work or personal, creating a standard others may not be able to return. If forgiveness, honesty, and consideration are not present, they work to bring them in. Without them, a relationship is not worthwhile. For anything to work with a person, the relationship has to work. When there is conflict, problems will have to be talked about and healed before going on. They tend to be open and sharing, and they expect others to self-disclose, especially in the interest of resolving issues. They have a way of getting others to feel at ease and open up.

In their close relationships, they put a lot of energy into nurturing the relationship. There is a constant search for the ideal relationship where there is both friendship and romance with someone they can share everything with, especially meaning and purpose. Sometimes they have a hard time separating from their ideal and objectivity eludes them. The more abrupt style of others often leads to hurt feelings, which they nurse internally. Their style is to easily communicate affection and appreciation with just the right message. Too much time alone leaves them needy, yet they need time to reflect on their own meaning and purpose too.

SELF-PORTRAIT
From Conversations with Envisioner Mentors

What's it like to be you?

I really believe everything happens for a reason, to everybody. I'm a human being, there are other human beings around me, and each of us is unique. I trust when something is going to take me to a higher level and I'll bring lots of people along with me—a constant quest of building a strong foundation of self and others from everything I learn. Relationships are about the higher purpose—there is a deep level that needs to be satisfied or there is no point—I need a unique connection or I am unsatisfied. I feel a responsibility to make a difference.

I am empathic. I just get a feeling about people. It's difficult to explain. I have the gift of being able to relate and meaningful communication is a major piece of my life and a major vehicle for growth. I'm good at working with people to improve their behavior and their lives. I'm described as someone who cares, who has an uncanny sense for knowing what others need or what they are about. When I talk to people I'm listening for their stories and their concerns and I experience the joy or stress with them. I remember what's uniquely descriptive of that individual, and I am good at giving praise and pointing out the gifts they bring to their world. If I get vibes that they are not comfortable developing the relationship the way I think it should be, I will back off, but I look for another clue to come back and develop it. What matters is working at making the relationship the best that it can be at whatever level it is, building depth into it.

Honesty is very important. Even if the truth is bad it adds to the depth of the relationship.

I hate unresolved conflict—it makes me sick and can stay with me until it's resolved—and I hate it when people are demeaned or mistreated. My heart goes out to them so I feel it's my responsibility to help, and I will fight on their behalf. It's just something I do, but it hasn't always worked. I end up telling the person what to do and then they do what they want regardless. If I'm really upset, I'll let myself calm down, figure out what I'm going to say, and then confront the situation. I am very careful and aware of my actions or words and what effect they will have on another person, and I am thankful to have learned to take the time to envision various interactions before they happen. I used to push, but now I'm more patient. I'm usually fair, open, and unbiased. I don't understand people who are insensitive to others needs or issues or thoughts or feelings. Either I don't want them in my life or I want to teach them how to care. It bugs me when people don't take the time to understand each other.

I usually put the relationship ahead of tasks I have to do, but I don't have unlimited energy. When I can just be who I am and in a sharing mode and when there is not a task-oriented pressure, that flows better. I try hard to "be there" emotionally for those in my life so I have to constantly set up boundaries so I don't take on their problems. I usually work overtime to make sure I am understood. It is also very important to me for others' to be properly understood, and I expend a lot of time and energy making sure they are understood and comfortable. Being unable to build relationships with those who need it is frustrating.

It's particularly difficult when my needs aren't being met. Sometimes I can't even feel good about myself because I worry that others did not get what they needed. In a group, I need to separate my interests from others or I'll be easily swayed by what they want and how they behave. I can't be successful for myself if I'm trying to fit into someone else's idea of me.

I also tend to take a leadership position—not a strong one always but I'm looked at as a leader. Others having genuine confidence in me is almost as good as having the confidence myself. When someone comes for help, it's a compliment. I listen and feed some things back that maybe they haven't thought about, something that's profound for them. Often people will disregard the information I give them as unimportant only to later request the same information. That energizes me. I try to be a thoughtful good listener, interested, fun, and someone to come up with ideas. Humor is a great teacher and great healer. My favorite thing is to watch someone have an "aha" experience, and I really admire people who have been through something and learned.

Foreseer Developer

TEMPERAMENT: IDEALIST
INTERACTION STYLE: CHART THE COURSE
PERSONALITY TYPE CODE: INFJ

SNAPSHOT

Theme is foresight. Use their insights to deal with complexity in issues and people, often with a strong sense of "knowing" before others know themselves. Talents lie in developing and guiding people. Trust their inspirations and visions, using them to help others. Thrive on helping others resolve deep personal and ethical dilemmas. Private and complex, they bring a quiet enthusiasm and industry to projects that are part of their vision.

PORTRAIT
Themes

For Foreseer Developers, life is a process of never-ending personal growth, their own and others'. If something does not produce personal growth, then it is not truly worthwhile. If it does, then it is indeed worth all the effort it takes to make that growth happen. They enjoy problem solving in ways that sustain the vision they have of what can be and who we can become. They devote their lives to honoring the gifts of others, helping them to see what those gifts are and to find a way to develop those gifts.

Taking a meaningful and creative approach to all aspects of life is essential to their well-being. This gives them the inner strength to allow others the space to be themselves and make the choices they make. It is then that their talent for foreseeing becomes painful. The hard part is that sometimes people don't want to hear all the insights they have to offer.

Interpersonally, exploring issues is important and navigating through all the emotions that make up relationships is essential.

Their thought processes tend to be highly integrative as they frequently become aware of the profound significance and interrelatedness of the many ideas, relationships, and events around them. When they allow themselves the space away from the hustle and bustle of day-to-day life, they often are conduits for profound symbols that speak to many. Symbols and metaphors come to them easily as ways to bridge differences and connect people with their potential. Yet they often find themselves engaging in quite practical problem solving, which doesn't begin to reveal the rich foresight behind the suggestions they offer and the agendas they set.

They live life with such a sense of purpose that they often present a very task-oriented side to the world that belies their more visionary, idealistic side. Such a life often presents them with a great deal of stress, which can cause them to withdraw from others to seek some sort of relief and recharge.

Relationships

For Foreseer Developers, relationships are about developing potential, their own and others'. They seem to tune in to the essence of the other person and take great pleasure in developing what they see there, usually by focusing on the positive aspects. They have a way of communicating that results in improvement and growth and often are disturbed when the negative is emphasized. They know what impact their words will have and don't want to say what they can't take back—always aware of the implications of the communications. They are usually able to manage their own emotions so well, others may perceive them as distant. While they don't like conflict, they won't avoid it if it can improve a relationship or lead to growth. Relationships are often forged around suggesting solutions to problems, and they feel validated when the other person finds them catalytic and helpful. They will work hard to avoid conflicts of interest; they must be ethical. It is difficult for them to be in relationships where they can't be who they truly are. While they may come into a relationship with expectations, they are often willing to change to meet new expectations.

Their close relationships are built on a strong vision of what a relationship will become, emotional intimacy, and shared values. They can be very intense, and their partner may not share their intensity. They can be playful but cautious. Their relationships are generally long and enduring. When the relationship is right, the commitment fulfills their highest purpose and they give it their all. Even though there is a strong empathic connection, there may still be a reserve and there always remains a piece that is private. Paradoxically, they need both solitude and connectedness.

SELF-PORTRAIT
From Conversations with Foreseer Developers

What's it like to be you?

The quest for more knowledge, the meaning of life, the philosophical questions—my mind is always occupied, and what's exciting is when I get to follow through with an insight and do something. I am an abstract future thinker, looking at things from different perspectives. I'm about the relationships and possibilities and enjoy anything with deeper meaning that leaves me wondering, with more questions to ask and things to untangle. Connecting for me means being able to intuitively ask questions of people to get them to go deeper into the things they are talking about.

Inspiring others, helping them find their purpose or meaning, being a different kind of leader from what's traditional—that's really gratifying. I just do that naturally. The challenge is opening up people's minds to have their own original thoughts. I'm a listener and guide.

I think I am a mystery to people. They never really understand me and part of me enjoys that. More often though, I long to be understood.

I tend to approach my day with a structured way of getting things accomplished. People see me as organized, thorough, and easy to get along with, pulling my own weight and eager to help out when called upon. But I'm not as outgoing or as critical as I may sometimes appear. I need a balance between people contact and working on creative projects and will break away from interactions when I get tired out. If I don't have some long-term goals, then what's the point?

I tend to intuitively read people very quickly, but I have to be cautious not to make assumptions. I'm an observer. I get a feeling when people are interesting, and I watch from a distance, make some assessments about the situation, and then approach them and engage in conversation. I put a little bit out and a little more and see how that goes. Do I trust and like them, are they who

they say? I have a few deep friendships. A friendship comes best when it is worked to develop that investment. I quickly pick up on sincerity and withdraw if the person is superficial or obviously doesn't care. When I see people who abuse their power or won't stand behind what they say, that ticks me off. It's about integrity. I feel other people's feelings, and taking on that burden can make me too intense and serious, where I can't be spontaneous and fun loving.

I like whatever gets us to think beyond the box, where people can function better because they are not afraid to say things they really feel. I have a lot of imagination and by and large can amuse myself. I love independent projects and reading and writing. I do my best thinking alone, and I like getting out in nature, being alone to go inside and center myself. I have always been drawn to the spiritual. Everywhere, I see life in symbols. Symbols give me focus. Sometimes the connections and perceptions in my mind are so abstract there are no words to explain. A lot of times I just know something and can't explain it—a premonition that's hard to articulate. If it's strong I usually say something or explore where it's coming from, but I will keep it to myself if people don't seem to understand. Informed decisions require lots of information and looking at a situation from as many different points of view as possible. I find it amusing, the absurdity in everyday situations.

It is painful when there is conflict or when I offer advice and someone chooses not to take it. For me, I have to prepare myself for what is going to happen so I can either support people in a positive way or get away and wait out the inevitable heavy duty stuff before returning to fix things. How will it impact me and the people in my life? Will it put me in another place or another level where I can grow more? Not knowing the right thing to say and do is stressful.

Everything revolves around growth. Caring is about the ability to help others grow. What I bring is caring about people, not things. If we spent more time trying to understand each other's point of view, to communicate more effectively, we would grow. In an honest, open, sincere relationship, I can accomplish anything. My challenge is to create those kinds of relationships. I respect most the person who is willing to come forth and be an individual—to make the world a better place, or make a difference in a person's life, where we reach each other's hearts.

Discoverer Advocate

TEMPERAMENT: IDEALIST
INTERACTION STYLE: GET THINGS GOING
PERSONALITY TYPE CODE: ENFP

SNAPSHOT

Theme is inspiration, both of themselves and others. Talents lie in grasping profound significance, revealing truths, and motivating others. Very perceptive of others' hidden motives and purposes. Interested in everything about individuals and their stories as long as they are genuine. Contagious enthusiasm for "causes" that further good and develop latent potential and the same zeal for disclosing dishonesty and inauthenticity. Frequently moved to enthusiastically communicate their "message."

PORTRAIT

Themes

For Discoverer Advocates, life is a process of inspiring and facilitating others to find and reach their full potential. They have a talent for seeing the core of someone, the unspoken essential goodness. They become the spokesperson for others, for what is needed most and for their higher purpose. They enjoy exploring perceptions and sharing deep emotional content, the "real stuff." This sharing is a magic moment when they truly connect. They constantly seek to have ideal relationships where they can have many ideal moments. To not have these empathic moments is like being cut off from themselves.

Life is like a story. Stories provide ways to find meaning and to make a difference and provide the connecting thread that helps them know and understand others and work through situations.

Their thought processes seem random; however, they are connective and relational. They are able to mediate differences and conflict by seeing the ways the differences connect. They often become the "voice" for the unspoken meanings they so easily pick up. They strive to keep communication channels open to make the best of a situation. They have a way of making things work without knowing why, which gives them the air of being magical as they respond courageously to their insights. The creative process is an important part of their lives.

In the interpersonal arena, they often instantly like people or not. Liking the people they are with is important. With their talent for seeing what's not being said, they often respond to others' needs while putting their own needs and wants on hold. They like to spark something in others that others don't see in themselves. They must be able to authentically live with themselves and seek to recognize happiness wherever it is.

They often feel a strong need to discover a definitive direction for themselves. They want the magical situation to be permanent so are paradoxically on a continual quest for direction, resulting in a feeling of unrest.

Relationships

For Discoverer Advocates, relationships are about being on the same wavelength. People often get the sense they are understood perfectly by them. They are so perceptive in the moment that they read and mirror the other person's mood, the meanings of the other person's behavior, and when they're on, they're really right and everything feels in sync. The downside is they can make a lot of assumptions and projections that are sometimes really wrong. They can establish rapport instantly, can be charming and flirtatious in a way that uniquely connects with the other person. They frequently do whatever it takes to understand the deep meaning in what others do. Others may feel strangely connected with them, as if they have known them forever, and yet know nothing about them. They are uncanny at being the center of attention without being the topic of conversation. Getting at deep issues is important to them, and in the process, they are often catalysts for change. They want everyone to engage.

In their close relationships, they are romanticizing and idealistic. They want to share interests, ideas, and activities. Their ideal is a twin-like relationship, participating with each other, sharing the experience of it, where the relationship is real-time, live and in-person, with each other's beliefs the same. When that ideal connection is not there, they can become disillusioned and disappointed. They are often supportive of their partner's efforts to develop his or her potential and want to be supported and nurtured in return.

SELF-PORTRAIT
From Conversations with Discoverer Advocates

What's it like to be you?

I have to be directly in contact with people and know that somehow I am influencing what happens for them in a positive way. That is a kind of driving force in my life, actualizing potential, giving encouragement, letting people know what I think they can do. I have been told I have this uncanny ability to absolutely zero in on and intuit what people need. I sometimes recognize something about them that they have not said to anybody else. And they say, "How did you know?"

I see myself as a facilitator. It's not about imposing what I want to see happen, although I have some grand ideal of everyone having a better life or feeling better or dealing with a particular issue. Being able to understand people in depth gives me a feeling I have been friends with them forever, and when I act too much that way, they may not be able to handle it. But I feel sad when I see potential in someone and they are either denying it or not able to access it in some way. I'm very sensitive too, but sometimes easily discouraged, and I still go on thrilled to meet new people, with an interest in assisting them in whatever they are seeking. I give them both knowledge and meaning. I bring a fresh perspective and my appreciation for people's goodness.

If I'm stuck for hours working at a monotonous task, I get peculiar, zonky, and weird. I get very tired if I can't get out and exchange information. I'll lack bounce, the bubbling of ideas that makes me run through life. I absolutely have to have a fulfilling job or I get depressed. I want to use my talents, make a difference, and have autonomy. If not, I struggle to retain a sense of self and it's like my spirit is dying.

People talk about being drawn to me. Friends are so important to me and I have good intentions. I like to think I'll do whatever I can do to hold on to them, but often I don't get around to writing or calling. They know that if they create a friendship with me, then the friendship is going to be intense and loyal and I will be there for them when they really need me. And I can engage with people that I care about who are a distance away and feel like they are a part of my life on an ongoing basis, picking up a lot of feeling from what they write or when they call. It would be easier to spin straw into gold than be totally alone.

As a kid I did a lot of imaginary things. It's like acting. I am very enthusiastic about many different things and very romantic. I have a child-like quality and like to get others roped into that too. Fun is a feeling of satisfaction as opposed to just an activity, the feeling of being able to smile all the time and get others to smile. What's fun is watching other people find out they can really do something they otherwise never thought of themselves as capable of doing.

I have a strong sense of ethics and fairness and I can be a little too aware of an imbalance. I am a perfect mimic. I can be someone else and get enormous insight about that person, and I want to tell them about it. I admire authenticity, the person who can just be, and speaking the truth with clarity and tact, to get this magic bond where we are transfixed in that moment. That's something I seek.

The way to tick me off is to either do something really unethical or question my integrity. I get very annoyed when people jump me for not doing things their way, but I often don't defend myself because I fear losing control. I'd rather be in control when I talk to them about the situation. They don't know what effect they're having and it tears me up inside. It makes me crazy if I am in conflict with someone who wants to walk away and I need to engage with them until we work it out. I need to be supported, not just always the giver and catalyst. And I need contact—emotional, intellectual, just words—for fun and connection.

I remember this wonderful little boy, but he was conning everyone. I kept looking straight at him, "in the soul," and finally he put his hands up over his eyes and said, "You've got to quit looking at me like that. I can look at people like that, but you can't look at me like that." And I completely understood him and I said, "I know who you are, and it's not bad. It's good, you're good, and you have promise." That's what people don't want to hear—I see you, I value you, I care what you'll become, and I wish to be a part of that if you need me.

Harmonizer Clarifier

TEMPERAMENT: IDEALIST
INTERACTION STYLE: BEHIND THE SCENES
PERSONALITY TYPE CODE: INFP

SNAPSHOT

Theme is advocacy and integrity. Talents lie in helping people clarify issues, values, and identity. Support anything that allows the unfolding of the person. Encourage growth and development with quiet enthusiasm. Loyal advocates and champions, caring deeply about their causes and a few special people. Interested in contemplating life's mysteries, virtues, and vices in their search for wholeness. Thrive on healing conflicts, within and between, and taking people to the center of themselves.

PORTRAIT
Themes

For Harmonizer Clarifiers, life is a process of uncovering mysteries, the mysteries of life—personal values and meanings and the meaning of life in general. They like learning about people, why they do what they do and who they are. They want to relate on a deep level, to be touched deeply and to resolve issues. Exploring moral questions like what is right and wrong and the battle between good and evil fascinates them. Knowing people's intentions helps them feel comfortable with their relationships.

They enjoy getting reacquainted with themselves. To not have a sense of congruence with their values and unity with oneself is worse than death. They must have a sense of integrity and wholeness.

They have a talent for facilitative listening and knowing what is behind what is said. When they listen deeply to another person, they help that person clarify their identity, their wants, and their needs. They want to help others enjoy who they are, accept themselves, and believe in themselves. Sometimes it is hard to turn off the deep listening, and they pay a price for presenting a more acceptable, conventional persona to the world.

Life is full of paradoxes and they are constantly balancing opposites. They can be fun and playful yet serious and intense. Others rarely glimpse the whole, rich tapestry of their lives. They often relate to others through stories and metaphors to connect differences and to provide gentle encouragement. Stories tap into that wordless internal world that is the source of knowing what is right and important.

Their thought processes tend to be relational and integrative. "Going with the flow" helps them connect the seemingly unconnectable, life's many opposites. They often start in the middle of an idea, grasping its importance, and love to have the freedom to flow from one thought to the next. They have a way of knowing what is believable.

Their incredible ability to be present with another on a deep level requires a different sense of time than structured time. They often speak of struggling with structure, forever trying to get their lives in order.

Relationships

For Harmonizer Clarifiers, relationships are about self-discovery—each person learning more about who he or she really is. There is an idealism in the process of relating, and everything has a symbolic significance. They want the other person, the group members, or the community to have a sense of purpose and ethics. They will just know when they are getting the "real" person in the relationship. Integrity, validation, and affirmation are very important. They can be an enigma, with many aspects of themselves for different relationships. Sharing beliefs is important. They are often disappointed if the other person or the group doesn't share their beliefs and will then tend to withdraw and be silent. There is a lot of self-reflectiveness about how to "be" in a relationship, and they may miss the moment for connecting; so much is internal, but they want so much to connect they may do it indirectly.

In their close relationships, they can be very subtle and are often the most romantic. Others may miss the significance of their symbolic gestures. When the other person is right with them, the person is totally right, and when the other person is not, then that person is totally wrong. They expect the relationship to be deep and meaningful. When it is, they are willing to commit.

SELF-PORTRAIT
From Conversations with Harmonizer Clarifiers

What's it like to be you?

I have a very internal focus. I think I look at myself through other people's eyes, but sometimes I can lose touch with how things work for me. Then I can get introspective, going very deep and staying there, not coming out too quickly or easily. Somehow I find it very difficult to put into words and communicate the things that really matter to me. Most people don't have the foggiest notion about what goes on with me.

I like harmony and seek consensus and do well with the deep issues. My values and the things that are important to me often feel outside the mainstream in the sense that I feel impinged upon and uncomfortable with so much of what goes on. I'm too private to push my values on to other people, but I am convinced that one ought to be congruent in their own life if they are going to expect congruence from others. In a sense I hold other people to that standard, and I worry about my own incongruities, inconsistencies, and contradictions. Groups can be hard. I can put myself in the group process so rapidly and so completely, and it's important not to get sucked in. I need to be predictable about what I believe.

I am a global thinker and I like to learn interactively. My thoughts need to be connected with some person or value. On reflection, don't all thoughts have to be connected to something? I feed new information into other things I've read and my thoughts, and I can have a marvelous time just sitting with ideas. And I like to discuss or write things because I seem to have a lot in my head and I've got to get it out. I love bringing together different eclectic ideas and seeing what's similar. I like to have my own ideas, hear others ideas, and have ideas challenged, bantering back and forth. Chitchat has no interest for me. I tend to do a lot of mental rehearsal and play in problem solving, and the fun part is figuring out how to do something. Motivation comes when something has real meaning or value for me, and while I enjoy ideas I don't like having my values challenged.

For me, asking questions is just a different form of being quiet, a way to explore an inner thought stream or check out of reality and back into my thoughts. Sometimes I chuckle at myself that there is really no sequential way that I work though tasks.

I have always trusted my intuition, even before I was aware of it. I enjoy talking to people. It's interesting to learn about them, where they're coming from and how they invent their reality. And I have an innate talent for reading between the lines—to hear what hasn't been said—and a sense of what needs to be said and done. I tend to form impressions right away about people, and most of the time I feel pretty good about my impressions but sometimes I am way off. At least if the people have good intentions, I can relax.

I enjoy seeing people enjoy who they are, and I get a lot of joy helping others discover that they have value. Being able to help someone in their darkest hour, to communicate across differences and find common ways of working together, that is very satisfying because then there is a real sense of closeness and acceptance and a genuine pursuit of helping people heal and achieve their goals. I hold on to relationships even though we may go long periods without seeing each other, and I cherish those long associations.

I'm concerned about how others feel when they are around me. Lack of honesty or ethics or integrity in interactions—when someone is saying one thing but doing another—really puts me off. So does when someone doesn't honor, or accept as valid, my communication or feeling as I try to talk to them about something that matters to me. And I don't need to talk about myself. I don't enjoy it. Sometimes I'm frustrated trying to communicate, and sometimes a metaphor or a joke or a story is a way to effectively express myself so what I'm saying can be heard by someone who hears or experiences things differently.

I don't know what I am going to do next, but I trust in myself that something will come in as a new idea, with challenge and inner meaning. Whatever it is, it will be right. Although I would never actually say it, it feels as though I am grounded in the very being of who I am when I talk like this.

Understanding Yourself

Based on what you have read and learned about yourself, complete the following statements and answer the question at the bottom of the page.

The Johari Window

	Known to Self	**Unknown to Self**
Known to Others	PUBLIC KNOWLEDGE **What others recognize as true of me . . .**	FEEDBACK **What I want to ask others to confirm as fitting me . . .**
Unknown to Others	PRIVATE **What I really want to let others know about me so they understand me . . .**	UNCONSCIOUS **Oh my gosh! That's really true! The things I didn't know about myself . . .**

Are there any characteristics in the descriptions that you've disowned because they were not valued by others? If so, what are they?

Action Plan

How will this new knowledge about yourself and others change how you relate to people? Use The Johari Window to create an action plan.

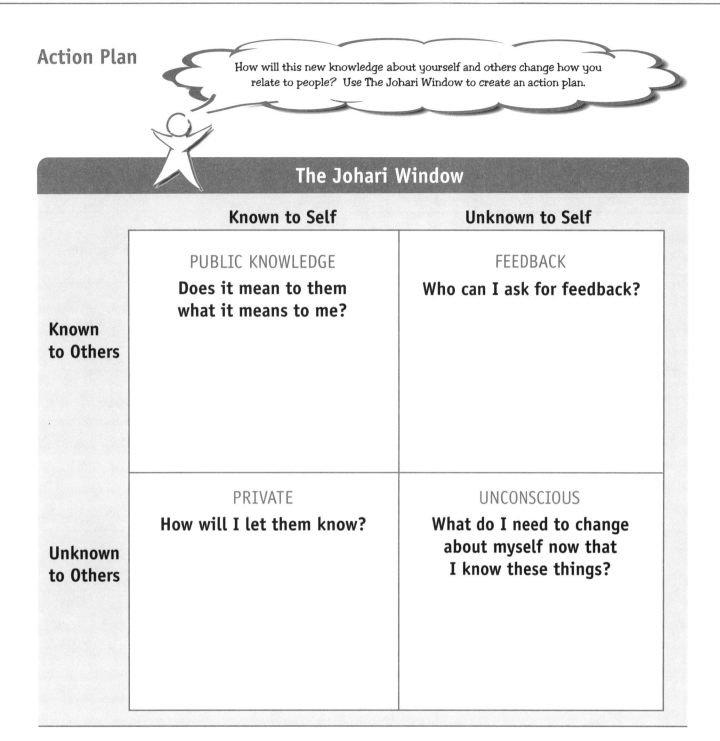

The Johari Window

	Known to Self	Unknown to Self
Known to Others	PUBLIC KNOWLEDGE **Does it mean to them what it means to me?**	FEEDBACK **Who can I ask for feedback?**
Unknown to Others	PRIVATE **How will I let them know?**	UNCONSCIOUS **What do I need to change about myself now that I know these things?**

What steps will you take to foster untapped talents or reclaim any disowned characteristics?

Relating to Others

Write down the names of the people in your life in the box that you think most represents their personality type pattern.

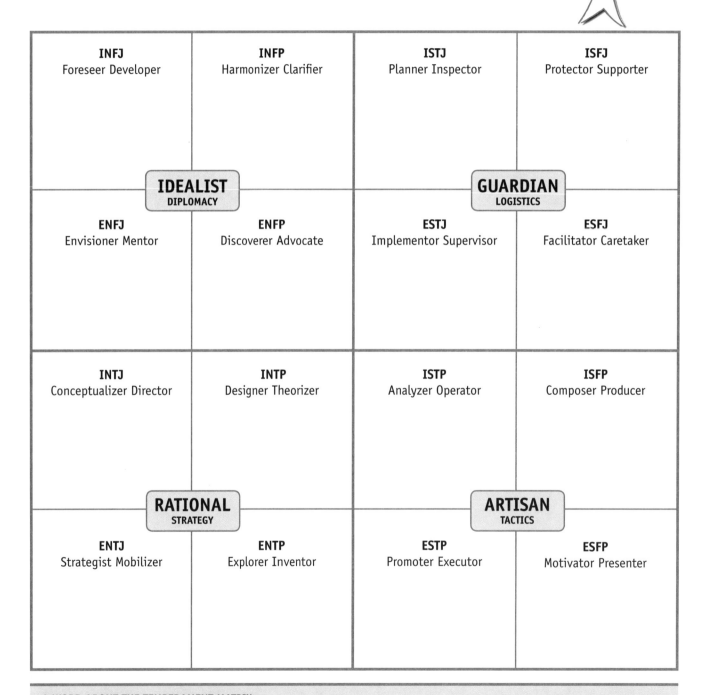

INFJ Foreseer Developer	**INFP** Harmonizer Clarifier	**ISTJ** Planner Inspector	**ISFJ** Protector Supporter
IDEALIST DIPLOMACY		**GUARDIAN** LOGISTICS	
ENFJ Envisioner Mentor	**ENFP** Discoverer Advocate	**ESTJ** Implementor Supervisor	**ESFJ** Facilitator Caretaker
INTJ Conceptualizer Director	**INTP** Designer Theorizer	**ISTP** Analyzer Operator	**ISFP** Composer Producer
RATIONAL STRATEGY		**ARTISAN** TACTICS	
ENTJ Strategist Mobilizer	**ENTP** Explorer Inventor	**ESTP** Promoter Executor	**ESFP** Motivator Presenter

A WORD ABOUT THE TEMPERAMENT MATRIX

The organizing principle of the matrix maintains four broader central temperament distinctions. The four temperament patterns and their subcategories are displayed in a matrix that is designed to make it is easy to see the interactional dynamics between people of different temperaments and types. See Appendix A for an explanation.

Now What?

> *Think of the people you noted on the previous page. Answer the following questions about them. Use these reflections to increase your own self-awareness and to improve your relationships.*

What do you like/dislike about the person? Review their type description.

Is what you like or dislike related to their type pattern? If so, how can you be more accepting of and actually appreciate the person?

Is what you dislike a projection of your own blind spots? If so, seek to find some value in that aspect of the person and allow yourself to not be as proficient in that area.

Is what you admire in the person, what you need to develop in yourself? Would the person make a good coach or role model for you?

What's Next?

You've found your *best-fit type*, so what do you do with it? Here are some tips to consider.

Find other sources of information to learn more about the characteristics of the type patterns in general. A lot of books are available that give more comprehensive descriptions. There are professionals around the world who use these models in their work. There is even a membership organization where "type" is the focus.

Use your new self-knowledge to empower yourself, to take charge of your life.

- Find a more satisfying career that engages your gifts or one that challenges you to develop.
- Assert yourself; seek out what is most important to you.
- Reclaim disowned qualities.
- Be more patient with yourself.
- Appreciate and celebrate who you are.

Use your new understanding of others to create more success in all of your relationships—work and personal. Each individual will define success differently and will have a different way of knowing when he or she is being successful.

What are your definitions of success?

> *Find the music in yourself; enjoy your melody. Listen to the music in others; enjoy the ensemble—whether it is a duet, a quartet, or an orchestra.*

Essential Qualities of the Personality Patterns

We use three lenses to look at the sixteen types—Temperament, Interaction Styles, and Cognitive Dynamics. Each lens provides different information about personality. Sometimes it is useful to explore each lens on its own. Other times two lenses are used together for a more complete picture. The three lenses taken together give the fullest picture and provide the most information.

Temperament

(For a complete explanation of Temperament Theory, see the References for *Understanding Yourself and Others®: An Introduction to Temperament*.)

Temperament Theory is based in descriptions of behavior that go back over twenty-five centuries. It tells us the "why" of behavior, our motivators, and sources of deep psychological stress. Knowing our temperament patterns tells us our core needs and values as well as the talents we are more likely to be drawn to develop. Temperament gives us four broad themes in a pattern of core psychological needs, core values, talents, and behaviors—all of which are interrelated.

The four temperament patterns also have qualities in common with each other and can be described in those terms as well.

Abstract versus Concrete language—the way we tend to think about things and the way we use words. The Idealist and Rational patterns are characterized by abstract language with a focus on intangibles—concepts, ideas, implications, and meaning. People with these patterns as primary seek to know or explain the meaning of something that is not seen in order to access information that is not obvious. The Guardian and Artisan temperament patterns are characterized by concrete language with a focus on tangibles—experiences and observations. Those with these patterns seek to get or give useful concrete information to plan for the future of take action in the present.

Affiliative versus Pragmatic roles—the way we prefer to interact with others. The Idealist and Guardian patterns are more Affiliative in nature, with a focus on interdependence, human and group effectiveness, inclusion, agreement, and sanction. The Rational and Artisan patterns are more Pragmatic in nature with a focus on independence and operational effectiveness, self-determination, autonomous actions, and expedience.

Another dimension not shown on the matrix is the focus on Structure versus Motive—where we focus our attention when interacting with others. The Rational and Guardian patterns are characterized by a focus on structure, order, and organization to gain a measure of control over life's problems and irregularities rather than be at the mercy of random forces. The Idealist and Artisan patterns are characterized by a focus on motives and why people do things in order to work with the people they are communicating with rather than trying to force them into a preconceived structure.

Of the three lenses, temperament is the broadest and each temperament pattern describes the driving force of four of the sixteen types.

Interaction Styles

(For a complete explanation of Interaction Styles, see the References for *Understanding Yourself and Others®: An Introduction to Interaction Styles*.)

Interaction Styles is based on observable behavior patterns that are quite similar to the popular social styles models and DISC®. Interaction Styles tells us the "how" of our behavior. It refers to patterns of interaction that are both highly contextual and yet innate. Knowing our interaction style helps us locate interpersonal conflicts and situational energy drains. It gives us a map for greater flexibility in our interactions with others.

These four interaction style patterns are characterized by different interactional dynamics. Those dynamics are Directing/Informing and Initiating/Responding.

The *Directing* style has a time and task focus with a tendency to direct the actions of others to accomplish a task in accordance with deadlines, often by either telling or asking. Regarding motivations and process, the Directing style is explicit.

The opposite style is *Informing*, with a motivation and process focus. Using this style, people tend to give information in order to enroll others in the process. When a task needs to be accomplished, the Informing style engages others, describing outcomes and processes that can be used to complete the task.

Each style has its own best and appropriate use, and most people use both at different times but have more comfort with one.

Each of these patterns can also be further differentiated by another dimension—a preference for either *Initiating* interactions and a faster pace or for *Responding* to interactions and a slower pace. The four different interaction style patterns are shown in the matrix below.

The Four Interaction Style Patterns

	DIRECTING	INFORMING
RESPONDING	**CHART-THE-COURSE** DIRECTING/RESPONDING Push for a plan of action Keep the group on track Deliberate decisions Define the process focus	**BEHIND-THE-SCENES** INFORMING/RESPONDING Push for the best result Support the group's process Consultative decisions Understand the process focus
INITIATING	**IN-CHARGE** DIRECTING/INITIATING Push for completion Lead the group to the goal Quick decisions Results focus	**GET-THINGS-GOING** INFORMING/INITIATING Push for involvement Facilitate the group's process Enthusiastic decisions Interaction focus

Cognitive Dynamics

(For a complete explanation of Cognitive Dynamics, see the reference for *Dynamics of Personality Type: Understanding and Applying Jung's Cognitive Processes.*)

Cognitive Dynamics is based in the Jungian theory from which psychological type instruments are derived. Each of the sixteen types has a theme based in a unique dynamic pattern of cognitive processes and their development. Knowing our innate tendencies to use these processes in certain ways can help us release blocks to our creativity and to effective communication. This model provides us the key to growth and development.

Carl Jung's Theory of Psychological Type

In examining individual differences, Swiss psychiatrist Carl Jung differentiated two fundamentally different orientations. He noticed some people seem primarily oriented to the world outside themselves. He called these people *extraverted*. He saw other people as primarily oriented to the world inside themselves. He called these people *introverted*. This extraverted-introverted difference is related to where you focus and recharge your energy. Then Jung noticed that people could be further distinguished by their preferred mental processes. Jung saw two kinds of mental processes used in everyday life: the process of *perception* (becoming aware of) and the process of *judgment* (organizing or deciding).

He then further differentiated two kinds of perception—*Sensation* and *Intuition*. *Sensing* is a process of

becoming aware of sensory information. *Intuiting** is a process of becoming aware of abstract pattern information and meanings. Both kinds of information are available to us, but we pay attention to only one kind at a time. Both are necessary and valuable in everyday life.

Likewise, he noted two kinds of judgment—*Thinking* and *Feeling*. Thinking judgments are based on objective criteria and are detached from personal values. Feeling judgments are based on subjective considerations and are attached to personal and universal values. Even the smallest act involves either Thinking or Feeling judgments, and both kinds of decisions are needed and valuable.

Each of these four mental processes can be used in either the external world of extraversion or the internal world of introversion, producing eight mental processes. Then Jung outlined eight psychological types, each characterized by the predominance of one of these eight mental processes (extraverted Sensing, introverted Sensing, extraverted iNtuiting, introverted iNtuiting, extraverted Thinking, introverted Thinking, extraverted Feeling, and introverted Feeling). In his writings he suggested that each of these eight dominant mental processes was supported by one of two opposing processes and that each of these eight types might vary according to which opposite mental process was used in support of the dominant. For example, the extraverted Sensing type with Thinking would be somewhat different from the extraverted Sensing type with Feeling. Thus, his notions imply sixteen type patterns, each characterized by preferences for the use of two of the eight mental *processes,* as shown in the table on the following page..

Enter Measurement and the Four-Letter Code

When Isabel Myers began developing the MBTI®, she faced several challenges. One challenge was the beginning of the self-report movement. Prior to that time, psychologists doubted that a self-report format would work. Also, it was a time of "measurement," and the scientific thinking of the time was to understand the world by dividing it into parts. Myers faced the challenge of keeping the holistic quality of Jung's types in the forefront, while meeting the demands of the tests and measurement world. She chose to focus on the opposites in Jung's theory. Jung said that the orientations of extraversion and introversion were dynamically opposite. You can't be in two places at one time! He also said the mental processes were dynamically opposite. Thus, one would have a preference for either Sensing or iNtuiting and Thinking or Feeling in one's day-to-day interactions. The genius of Isabel Myers (and her mother, Katharine Briggs) was to develop questions about everyday actions and choices that reflected these underlying opposing preferences.

When the preferences for each of these pairs of opposites were indicated, then the type pattern could be inferred.

---

* We use *Sensing* and *Intuiting* to refer to mental processes rather than *Sensation* and *Intuition,* which refer to names of something. Our focus is on the activity, not the "type."

The Four Sensing Types

extraverted **Sensing**	with	introverted Thinking	(ESTP)
extraverted **Sensing**	with	introverted Feeling	(ESFP)
introverted **Sensing**	with	extraverted Thinking	(ISTJ)
introverted **Sensing**	with	extraverted Feeling	(ISFJ)

The Four iNtuiting Types

extraverted **iNtuiting**	with	introverted Thinking	(ENTP)
extraverted **iNtuiting**	with	introverted Feeling	(ENFP)
introverted **iNtuiting**	with	extraverted Thinking	(INTJ)
introverted **iNtuiting**	with	extraverted Feeling	(INFJ)

The Four Thinking Types

introverted **Thinking**	with	extraverted Sensing	(ISTP)
introverted **Thinking**	with	extraverted iNtuiting	(INTP)
extraverted **Thinking**	with	introverted Sensing	(ESTJ)
extraverted **Thinking**	with	introverted iNtuiting	(ENTJ)

The Four Feeling Types

introverted **Feeling**	with	extraverted Sensing	(ISFP)
introverted **Feeling**	with	extraverted iNtuiting	(INFP)
extraverted **Feeling**	with	introverted Sensing	(ESFJ)
extraverted **Feeling**	with	introverted iNtuiting	(ENFJ)

However, a difficulty remained in how to determine which mental process was dominant in the personality and which was auxiliary. Myers reasoned that we can more readily observe what we do externally, so she decided to add questions to try to find which preferred mental process individuals used in the external world. If they used their preferred judging process to order the external world, they would be likely to make lists and structure their time in advance. If they used their preferred perceiving process to experience the external world, they would avoid such planning and structuring and prefer to keep things open-ended. Thus, the Judging-Perceiving scale of the MBTI was born. The resultant four-letter personality type code is used around the world to give people insights about themselves.

Type Dynamics and Development

Type dynamics is based on the theories of Carl Jung and refers to a hierarchy of cognitive processes (Sensing, iNtuiting, Thinking, Feeling) and a preference for being either in the external world (extraversion) or the internal world (introversion). Type dynamics and type development refer to the unfolding of the personality pattern as expressed through the development of the mental processes of perception and judgment. Since the personality is a living system, it is self-organizing—self-maintaining, self-transcending, and self-renewing. Growth and development follow principles of organic development, and there is an order to the evolution of the personality.

The first cognitive process to develop and become more refined is often called the dominant. It is the favorite. The second is often called the auxiliary because it "helps" the first one. It develops second (usually between the ages of twelve to twenty). Development of the third

process usually begins around age twenty and continues until age thirty-five or so. The fourth or least preferred process usually comes into play more between the ages of thirty-five to fifty. These developmental ages are general, not fixed. At these times, we find ourselves drawn to activities that engage and utilize the processes.

Thus we can say that development is dynamic and growing. Development in this sense is like readiness to learn to talk or to walk. We don't have to make children do these, we only need to provide models and opportunities and then stay out of the way. Development can be diverted due to environmental pressures and so is not always in this order as we develop some "proficiencies" using these cognitive processes. Still, the innate preference pattern will remain the same.

How Do the Models Relate?

The temperament patterns (extended out to the four variations of each) meet Jung's theory at the level of the sixteen type patterns. The four-letter codes produced by the MBTI, when they are accurate and verified for individuals, match Keirsey's sixteen type patterns. While at first glance the matching process looks illogical, it occurs at a deep theoretical level when comparing Jung's and Kretschmer's original works. More importantly, it occurs on a descriptive, behavioral level. Following, is The Temperament Matrix with the sixteen themes, Interaction Styles, the four-letter personality type codes, and the type dynamics patterns represented by the type code. (The dominant is listed first, auxiliary second, tertiary third, and inferior fourth.)

The Temperament Matrix

		ABSTRACT		CONCRETE	
		Directing	**Informing**	**Directing**	**Informing**
AFFILIATIVE	**Responding**	Foreseer Developer *Chart-the-Course* INFJ $N_i\ F_e\ T_i\ S_e$	Harmonizer Clarifier *Behind-the-Scenes* INFP $F_i\ N_e\ S_i\ T_e$	Planner Inspector *Chart-the-Course* ISTJ $S_i\ T_e\ F_i\ N_e$	Protector Supporter *Behind-the-Scenes* ISFJ $S_i\ F_e\ T_i\ N_e$
			IDEALIST		**GUARDIAN**
	Initiating	Envisioner Mentor *In-Charge* ENFJ $F_e\ N_i\ S_e\ T_i$	Discoverer Advocate *Get-Things-Going* ENFP $N_e\ F_i\ T_e\ S_i$	Implementor Supervisor *In-Charge* ESTJ $T_e\ S_i\ N_e\ F_i$	Facilitator Caretaker *Get-Things-Going* ESFJ $F_e\ S_i\ N_e\ T_i$
PRAGMATIC	**Responding**	Conceptualizer Director *Chart-the-Course* INTJ $N_i\ T_e\ F_i\ S_e$	Designer Theorizer *Behind-the-Scenes* INTP $T_i\ N_e\ S_i\ F_e$	Analyzer Operator *Chart-the-Course* ISTP $T_i\ S_e\ N_i\ F_e$	Composer Producer *Behind-the-Scenes* ISFP $F_i\ S_e\ N_i\ T_e$
			RATIONAL		**ARTISAN**
	Initiating	Strategist Mobilizer *In-Charge* ENTJ $T_e\ N_i\ S_e\ F_i$	Explorer Inventor *Get-Things-Going* ENTP $N_e\ T_i\ F_e\ S_i$	Promoter Executor *In-Charge* ESTP $S_e\ T_i\ F_e\ N_i$	Motivator Presenter *Get-Things-Going* ESFP $S_e\ F_i\ T_e\ N_i$

Notes for the Facilitator

For the Type Knowledgeable

Background

We've explained some of the theoretical underpinnings in the text, but you may want to know more about how these descriptions were developed. We come from the perspective that there seem to be sixteen type patterns that have been recognized by many over the centuries. In the 1920s, Carl Jung, Ernst Kretschmer, Eduard Spränger, and others developed theories that eventually led to descriptions of these sixteen patterns. Isabel Myers, in her creative genius, made Jung's work available to everyone, not only through the development of the MBTI® but also through her insightful descriptions of the sixteen types. Independently, David Keirsey, in his creative genius, made Kretschmer's and Spränger's works available to everyone through the development of temperament theory. He recognized Myers's contributions and linked temperament theory and its sixteen patterns to her descriptions. Their contributions have worked synergistically to give people tools to use for better communication and relationships.

Gestalts

The descriptions were not "built" conceptually, using temperament principles, the preferences of the MBTI®, or Jung's functions in their attitudes. They were written as gestalts—themes or whole patterns not explainable by a sum of the parts. The theories were used as observational tools for getting as close as possible to the actual features, processes, and themes of the type. For example, consider ISTP and INTP. They are often described as very similar because they are alike in their dominant function (introverted Thinking) and different in their auxiliary functions. They are of different temperaments and different interaction styles. While there is evidence of dominant introverted Thinking, auxiliary extraverted Sensing, and the Artisan temperament in the ISTP themes, these models did not drive the construction of the descriptions. Our approach has been to identify themes unique to each type and describe them in terms that people of each type relate to, not how they would be described by the theories individually. Then, ISTPs will be most attracted to the ISTP descriptions and repelled by the INTP descriptions as well as all others. Theory-derived descriptions would not put "acting on hunches and intuitions" as a theme, because those words are used to describe the preferences of those with a preference for N. Yet in reality, this is how

ISTPs see themselves independent of learning about type. Although using type dynamics, since they have Intuition as their third function, it, too, is part of their pattern.

Psychologically Appealing

The descriptions were written to appeal to people of the type pattern. They are not meant to explain the type pattern but try to capture its essential characteristics. For example, one of the ESFP's themes is "Opening up people to possibilities." In type theory, "possibilities" is one of the descriptors of people with a preference for Intuition. Yet, ESFPs frequently describe themselves as seeing possibilities. These might be possibilities for actions to take, but especially for actions people can take to make their lives better.

The language of the descriptions should not be used to explain or characterize the type patterns. Every word was carefully chosen and if taken out of context is likely to misinform.

Facilitation Hints

Here are some hints for how to effectively use these descriptions to help clients and workshop participants find their *best-fit type*:

- Using activities or dialog, help them generate several hypotheses of which two or three type patterns are likely to fit.

- Help them remember that the results of the MBTI® are only one data source.

- Have them read these descriptions as a whole, paying attention to how they feel when they read them.

- Have them "try on" descriptions by reading the self-portrait out loud, so they can see if the language matches theirs.

- Try to emphasize the idea of the whole pattern, not just the number of characteristics that fit.

We wrote this booklet to use ourselves in facilitating The Self-Discovery Process℠. Like surveyors trying to accurately pinpoint a location, we have found taking several data points (triangulation) useful. In a typical feedback session or workshop, we are constantly checking against the following three models, using multiple data points and sources (like the MBTI®): (1) Temperament Theory without reference to the MBTI®, (2) Interaction Styles, and (3) Jungian Mental Processes, Type Dynamics, and Type Development. We hope the descriptions are helpful to you no matter what methods you use to help people clarify their types. Please call us with any feedback or questions you may have.

Temperament

Berens, Linda V., *Understanding Yourself and Others®: An Introduction to Temperament 2.0*. Huntington Beach, Calif.: Telos Publications, 2000.

Delunas, Eve. *Survival Games Personalities Play*. Carmel, Calif.: SunInk Publications, 1992.

Keirsey, David, and Marilyn Bates. *Please Understand Me*. 3d ed. Del Mar, Calif.: Prometheus Nemesis Books, 1978.

Keirsey, David. *Please Understand Me II*. Del Mar, Calif.: Prometheus Nemesis Books, 1998.

Keirsey, David. *Portraits of Temperament*. Del Mar, Calif.: Prometheus Nemesis Books, 1987.

Kretschmer, Ernst. *Physique and Character*. London: Harcourt Brace, 1925.

Nardi, Dario. *Multiple Intelligences and Personality Type: Tools and Strategies for Developing Human Potential*. Huntington Beach, Calif.: Telos Publications, 2001.

Roback, A. A. *The Psychology of Character*. New York: Arno Press, [1927]1973.

Spränger, E. *Types of Men*. New York: Johnson Reprint Company, [1928]1966.

Interaction Styles

Alessandra, Tony, and Michael J. O'Connor. *The Platinum Rule, Discover the Four Basic Business Personalities—and How They Can Lead You to Success*. New York: Warner Books, 1996.

Berens, Linda V., *Understanding Yourself and Others®: An Introduction to Interaction Styles*. Huntington Beach, Calif.: Telos Publications, 2001.

Bolton, Robert, and Dorothy Grover Bolton. *People Styles at Work: Making Bad Relationships Good and Good Relationships Better*. New York: American Management Association, 1996.

Bolton, Robert, and Dorothy Grover Bolton. *Social Style/Management Style: Developing Productive Work Relationships*. New York: American Management Associations, 1984.

Geier, John G. and Dorothy E. Downey. *Energetics of Personality*,.Minneapolis: Aristos Publishing House, 1989.

Geier, John G. and Dorothy E. Downey. *Personality Analysis*. Minneapolis: Aristos Publishing House, 1989.

Hunsaker, Phillip L. and Anthony J. Alessandra. *The Art of Managing People*. New York: Simon and Schuster, 1986.

Marston, William Moulton. *Emotions of Normal People*. Minneapolis: Persona Press, [1928]1979.

Tannen, Deborah. *You Just Don't Understand*. New York: William Morrow and Company, 1990.

Watzlawick, Paul; Janet Helmick Beaven and Don D. Jackson. *Pragmatics of Human Communication: A Study of Interactional Patterns, Pathologies, and Paradoxes*. New York: W.W. Norton and Company, 1967.

The 16 Personality Types

Baron, Renee. *What Type Am I?* New York: Penguin Putnam, 1998.

Berens, Linda V., et al. *Quick Guide to the 16 Personality Types, Understanding Personality Differences in the Workplace*. Huntington Beach, Calif.: Telos Publications, 2002.

Fairhurst, Alice M., and Lisa L. Fairhurst. *Effective Teaching, Effective Learning*. Palo Alto, Calif.: Consulting Psychologists Press, 1995.

Isachsen, Olaf, and Linda V. Berens. *Working Together: A Personality Centered Approach to Management*. 3d edition. San Juan Capistrano, Calif.: Institute for Management Development, 1991.

Nardi, Dario. *Character and Personality Type: Discovering Your Uniqueness for Career and Relationship Success*. Huntington Beach, Calif.: Telos Publications, 1999.

Segal, Marci. *Creativity and Personality Type: Tools for Understanding and Inspiring the Many Voices of Creativity*. Huntington Beach, Calif.: Telos Publications, 2001.

Jung/Myers Model

Berens, Linda V. *Dynamics of Personality Type: Understanding and Applying Jung's Cognitive Processes*. Huntington Beach, Calif.: Telos Publications, 1999.

Jung, Carl G. *Psychological Types*. Princeton, N.J.: Princeton University Press, 1971.

Myers, Isabel Briggs, with Peter B. Myers. *Gifts Differing*. Palo Alto, Calif.: Consulting Psychologists Press, [1980]1995.

Myers, Isabel Briggs, Mary H. McCaulley and Naomi L. Quenk. *MBTI Manual: A Guide to the Development and Use of the Myers-Briggs Type Indicator*. Palo Alto, Calif.: Consulting Psychologists Press, 1998.

Sharp, Daryl. *Personality Type: Jung's Model of Typology*. Toronto, Canada: Inner City Books, 1987.

Quenk, Naomi. *In the Grip*. Palo Alto, Calif.: Consulting Psychologists Press, 1985.

Biological Basis of Behavior

Chess, Stella, and Alexander Thomas. *Goodness of Fit: Clinical Applications from Infancy Through Adult Life*. Brunner Mazel, 1999.

Colt, George Howe. "Life Special: Were You Born That Way?" *Life* (April 1998): 38–50.

Hamer, Dean, and Peter Copeland. *Living with Our Genes: Why They Matter More Than You Think*. New York: Bantam Doubleday Dell, 1998.

Ornstein, Robert. *The Roots of the Self: Unraveling the Mystery of Who We Are*. San Francisco: HarperCollins, 1993.

Cultural Influences

Hofstede, Geert. *Culture and Organizations: Software of the Mind*. New York: McGraw-Hill, 1997.

Systems Thinking

Bateson, Gregory. *Mind and Nature: A Necessary Unity*. New York: Bantam Books, 1979.

Bateson, Gregory. *Steps to an Ecology of Mind*. New York: Ballantine Books, 1972.

Capra, Fritjof. *The Web of Life*. New York: Anchor Books, Doubleday, 1996.

Goldstein, Kurt. *The Organism*. New York: Zone Books, 1995.

Oshry, Barry. *Seeing Systems: Unlocking the Mysteries of Organizational Life*. San Francisco: Berrett-Koehler Publishers, 1996.

Wheatley, Margaret J. *Leadership and the New Science*. San Francisco: Berrett-Koehler Publishers, 1992.

Applying Multiple Models

Nardi, D., and L. Berens. "Wizards in the Wilderness and the Search for True Type." *Bulletin of Psychological Type* 21, no. 1 (1998). (This article is available on the Temperament Research Institute Web site—http://www.tri-network.com/articles/)

On the Internet

Temperament Research Institute, http://www.tri-network.com

Telos Publications, http://www.telospublications.com

Understanding Yourself and Others® Series

http://www.telospublications.com/uyao_series/